CLIMBING

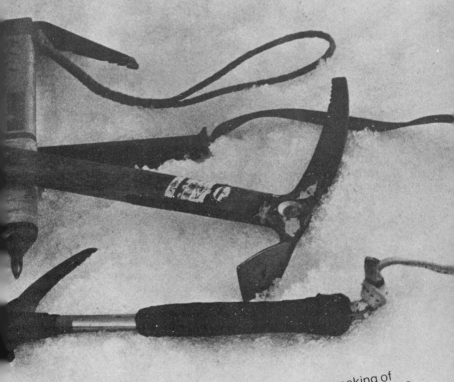

CLIMBING

JAMES BUNTING

THOMAS Y. CROWELL COMPANY
New York/Established 1834

Acknowledgements

All photographs in this book were taken by
John Cleare with the exception of the following:

Camera Press 38mr; J. Alan Cash 10, 18, 33
34–35; C. M. Dixon 48bL; Geological Survey
Denver Colorado 24; Keystone 19; Mansell
Collection 14; Meteorological Office Bracknell
38tL, tr, mL, bL, br; Doug Scott 48–49b; Picture-
point 40–41; Tony Smythe 36; UPI 19; Paul
Watkins 49b colour

L.C. Card 73-13113

Design by Paul Watkins & Florianne Henfield

Illustration Research by Susan Mayhew

Drawings by Len Bedford & Jacqueline Wright

Phototypeset by Oliver Burridge Filmsetting Limited,
Crawley, Sussex
Printed in Japan by Dai Nippon Printing Company

ISBN 0-690-00427-3

INTRODUCTION

It is curious how many people, right from their early childhood, have an insatiable desire to explore deep holes or to climb high mountains. Show a small boy the trench you have dug in the garden and he'll be in it like a flash; take him out into the country and, if there isn't a hillock for him to tackle, you'll find him clambering up a tree. In the days of primitive man this behaviour was undoubtedly instinctive, a means of isolating one's self from one's enemies and attackers. Today, potholing and climbing have found their way into the realms of sport and, like many other sports, they involve considerable physical training and the use of scientific techniques.

This book deals solely with the various aspects of climbing, ranging from the comparatively leisurely activity known as fell-walking to the grim realities of ascending sheer rock faces, some of which may be well over a thousand feet in height. It has been written not for the experts but for those who have had little or no climbing experience up to now and have always wanted to 'have a go'.

Above all else, the author realizes from his own practical experience that serious climbing is always fraught with hazards and, if attempted by persons without the necessary qualifications, can sometimes result in tragedy. Great care has therefore been taken not only to emphasize what degrees of physical and mental expertise are required in the individual climber, but also to discourage those who, by their own showing, can never make the grade.

By this means, it is hoped that the book will recruit many more enthusiasts to what, in the author's opinion, is one of the most exhilarating sports in the world and, at the same time, help to eliminate the sort of accidents that in recent years have tended to give climbing a bad name.

1 IN THE BEGINNING

Curious though it may seem, climbing as a sport owes its existence to religion, science and the arts.

In pagan times, those seeking to propitiate the gods would make their way, often with considerable difficulty, to the highest spot in the locality and there erect an altar on which to offer a sacrifice. They believed, as millions still do to this day, that the Deity existed somewhere in the sky and their aim was to get as close as possible. On the occasion of a special religious festival, the young men would vie with one another to build great bonfires on the summits of hills and mountains, hoping that the smoke would carry their prayers to heaven.

We find countless references to the sanctity of mountains in the Old Testament. For instance, Moses was told to serve God on a mountain and it was, of course, on top of a mountain that he received the Ten Commandments. In the twenty-third chapter of Deuteronomy these words are written: 'They shall call the peoples unto the mountains; there they shall offer sacrifices of righteousness.'

With the coming of Christianity, many early missionaries taking the Gospel from Rome into Central Europe risked their lives and endured appalling hardships in order to place crosses or erect shrines on high peaks in the alpine regions. Today many aids and a lot of sophisticated equipment are at the disposal of the climber. It seems miraculous that these monks—often bare-footed and

helped only by a stout stick—could achieve what most men would then have considered the impossible.

For several centuries the Catholic priests in Switzerland and northern Italy used climbing as a form of penance. A man found guilty of a grave sin was ordered by his parish priest to climb to the top of a mountain carrying a heavy wooden cross on his back. This he would have to plant on the summit so that it might be clearly visible from below and only on returning safely from completing this task would he be granted absolution. Early Swiss writings carry such accounts. Obviously many unfortunate people must have perished whilst undertaking their penance for they were never seen again. Traces of the penitential crosses are still to be found in the Alps, together with more recent crosses and cairns that were erected by the pioneers of mountaineering.

Early mountain climbers

Scientists began to take a keen interest in mountains in the late seventeenth century, since they believed they could learn from them many hitherto undiscovered facts about the earth's origin. But it was not until a hundred years later that they made any serious attempt to climb to high altitudes. In the summer of 1760 there arrived in the French Alpine village of Chamonix a brilliant science student from Geneva, Horace Benedict de Saussure. Although only twenty he had written many learned works.

De Saussure was fascinated by Mont Blanc, which was clearly visible from his home town, and his purpose in coming to Chamonix was to study the mountain at closer quarters. He tried three times to climb as far as the glaciers but sheer exhaustion forced him to give up. Nevertheless, he was convinced that it would be possible to reach the summit and, before returning to Geneva, he offered a prize to whoever got there first. It was not much of a prize— equivalent to no more than ten dollars—but in those days it represented the monthly earnings of a French peasant.

Yet it was not a peasant but another inhabitant of Geneva who first took up the challenge. Marc-Theodore Bourrit, a young man who had written several books and articles about the Alps, was as much obsessed with Mont Blanc as was de Saussure himself. But he lacked both stamina and courage. During the ten years following the offer of the reward he made three attempts to scale the mountain—taking de Saussure with him on one occasion— but never got within 6,000 feet of the 15,781-foot summit. After this de Saussure increased the reward money to ten times the original amount and eight years later, in 1783, it was announced that the doctor in Chamonix, Michel-Gabriel Paccard, was preparing to make the ascent. Bourrit, despite his previous failures, was still determined to get to the top first and suggested accompanying the doctor. They set out together in July but, the moment they reached the great Bossons Glacier, Bourrit lost his nerve and refused to go on the ice. Paccard continued for a short while alone —a foolhardy procedure—and then his better sense prevailed and the two returned to Chamonix.

A year later a local peasant, Jacques Balmat, accompanied by seven friends, tried to climb by another route. Balmat, who had a tougher constitution and a greater determination than the others, reached an altitude of 12,000 feet. Then, after enduring a night alone on the mountain, he too prudently decided to return. But his notable effort inspired Paccard and, early in August 1786, the doctor and Balmat set out again, this time together. On the evening of 8 August, at 6.30 pm precisely, they reached the summit.

Though Bourrit, green with envy, did his best to belittle the achievement, protesting that both men had lied about the climb, he was later disproved by a certain Baron von Gernsdorff, who had watched the ascent through a powerful telescope and who had definitely seen the figures of Paccard and Balmat standing on the summit. So their victory can be faithfully recorded as the first great achievement in climbing history.

De Saussure, who had started the ball rolling, made the third successful ascent in 1787 with eighteen villagers who later became Alpine guides. After that, Mont Blanc became the only peak to be climbed regularly for the next sixty years, with the Jungfrau, which had been conquered by the brothers Meyer of Aarau in 1811, becoming second favourite.

A photograph taken close to the summit of Mont Blanc. In the distance are the great peaks of the Pennine Alps—left to right—The Weisshorn, The Matterhorn and Monte Rosa

Balmat has sometimes been described as the father of mountaineering as a sport, but this honour should properly go to another scientist, Professor James David Forbes of Edinburgh. In 1833, when still in his twenties, he began touring the French Alps in search of botanical and geological specimens and, whilst exploring the mountains, he developed certain climbing techniques, some of which are still used today. He later wrote two notable books—*Travels Through the Alps of Savoy* (1843) and *Tour of Mont Blanc and Monte Rosa* (1855)—and their publication undoubtedly stimulated several thousands of people to take up climbing as a sport and was to some extent responsible for the formation of the English Alpine Club in 1857.

Strangely enough, the first president of this club was an Irishman, John Ball. He, too, was a scientist who loved travelling abroad, particularly in the Alps, and for a while he was one of Ireland's most distinguished politicians. Under his presidency the Club published its first volume of essays by its members in 1859, some of which contained further useful information on techniques, including advice on cutting steps in ice.

By now a number of prominent artists had been finding inspiration in climbers' country. The English Lake District, in particular, was attracting such famous painters as David Cox, Joseph Turner and James Whistler, and they and others, in order to do justice to the beautiful scenery, were carrying their easels and paint-boxes up into the mountains. They were among the first to discover the joys of hill walking (or, as they call it there, fell walking) and it is significant that when the first fell walkers' club was formed towards the end of the nineteenth century, nearly a third of its members were artists.

Edward Whymper

Artists were also beginning to invade the Alps, although few seem to have had the temerity to tackle the high peaks. However, from their ranks sprang a man who was without doubt the greatest climber of all in his day and age, Edward Whymper.

In 1854, when a boy of fourteen, Whymper had become apprenticed in his father's business of wood engraving. Six years later he had grown into such a talented artist that he was commissioned by Longman's, the London publishers, to do a series of illustrations for a book they were producing about the Swiss Alps. No sooner did he set eyes on his first high mountain than young Whymper was overwhelmed by a violent urge to climb to the top of it, the same urge that continues to make great mountaineers out of the most unlikely people. Indeed, Whymper was not at all the type of individual one would ever expect to become a climber. Slight in build, he possessed only moderate physical strength and was subject to recurrences of a chest trouble that had afflicted him in his early childhood.

Even so, he was able to make a few short climbs when he was touring the Dauphiné and the Berner Oberland. Then, on arriving at Zermatt in August, he found himself face to face with the Matterhorn and, at that very moment, knew that he must attempt its ascent even if he lost his life in the process. That risk was ever-present. The mountain had already killed or seriously injured nine climbers and there were those who maintained that its summit would never be reached, no matter from which side the assault was made. So far the only climbers who had met with any degree of success were Italians. They had made their ascents from their side of the Matterhorn, which had seemed to present fewer difficulties than the Swiss side, but their successive failures had by now reduced them to a state of despondency.

Whymper was astute enough to realize that he would need a lot more training and experience before making his attempt. In 1861 he spent two months climbing in the Lake District and the following year he went to Breuil, on the Italian side, being still of the opinion that the ascent would best be made from there. Five times he tried to reach the 14,782-foot summit, four times accompanied by a friend and once on his own, but was unable to make it. On his solo attempt he got to within 1,500 feet and injured himself seriously on the descent. Yet his resilience and enthusiasm were such that he was able to make his fourth and fifth climbs the following week.

In 1862 word reached Whymper that a very experienced climber and member of the Alpine Club, Professor Tyndall, had managed to get as far as the base of the 800-foot wall beneath the summit. In the following summer, he himself made a further essay from Breuil—this time with the Italian climber, Carrel, who for years had been determined to be first on the top—but they were beaten back by adverse weather. Whymper thereupon decided to make no further ascents from the Italian side but to try climbing from Zermatt. Despite this, he returned to Breuil in July 1865 and tried to enlist Carrel for a final attempt. At the eleventh hour, on 10 July, he received news that caused him great dismay. In Zermatt three other English climbers—the Rev. Charles Hudson and two young, inexperienced companions, the Lord Francis Douglas and Charles Hadow—had engaged two guides and were planning to tackle the Matterhorn on 13 July.

Whymper sped post-haste to Zermatt, secured the services of the only guide now available (Peter Taugwalder, the 22-year-old son of Lord Douglas's own guide) and, after much coercion, succeeded in joining forces with Hudson and his party. In the meantime, he informed them that Carrel, with two Italian climbers, would be simultaneously making an assault from Breuil. So it was to be neck or nothing.

In magnificent weather, the seven started out on the morning of 13 July and, after encountering surprisingly few hazards, they reached the summit at 1.40 on the following afternoon. Carrel had failed yet again but he succeeded in reaching the summit from the Italian side on 17 July.

Then came stark tragedy. On the way down, as they were descending a snowslope, Hadow missed his footing and fell. For a split second he was able to steady himself with the aid of the third guide, Michel Croz, then he slipped again, crashed down on to Croz and caused Hudson and Lord Douglas to lose their holds. Four men now hung suspended on the rope, held only by Whymper and the Taugwalders. The elder Taugwalder, number five on the rope, tried desperately to manoeuver Douglas (number four) to safety, but the rope suddenly broke and the four suspended men crashed to their deaths on the Matterhorn Glacier, nearly four thousand feet below. Three of the bodies were later recovered, but Douglas's remains have never been found.

The accident prompted certain ugly recriminations. It was said in one quarter that the rope had been bought cheaply by Whymper, was old and rotten and should never have been used. In another quarter, it was rumoured that, in order to save himself, his son and Whymper, the elder Taugwalder had cut the rope. A few even maintained that the rope had been cut on Whymper's orders. As the result of these allegations, Whymper lived under something of a cloud for the remainder of his days. Yet he will go down in history for his conquest of what was, in his day, the most feared peak in the Alps.

Nor was the Matterhorn his only outstanding triumph. After several climbs in the Caucasus he spent three years in the Andes and, in 1879, was the first man to reach the summit of the 20,450-foot Chimborazo in Ecuador. The feat was all the more remarkable in that it demonstrated that extra oxygen was not necessary.

The conquest of Mount Everest (29,028 feet), the highest mountain in the world, in 1953 was the greatest of all mountaineering achievements

Past and future achievements

The first notable North American peak to be scaled was Mount St. Elias (18,024 feet) in Alaska. Its summit was reached in 1897 by a party led by the 24-year-old Duke of Abruzzi who, three years later, beat Nansen's record in his Polar expedition. In 1897 also the 23,081-foot Aconcagua in Chile was conquered by the Swiss climber, Zurbriggen. The highest point of the North American continent, Mount McKinley, was reached by the Rev. Hudson Stuck, Archdeacon of the Yukon, on 23 June 1913, only a few days after Kain had attained the summit of the rocky Mount Robson in Alberta and not long before MacCarthy got to the top of another Yukon peak, Mount Logan.

But undoubtedly the greatest of all mountaineering achievements was the conquest of Everest. Its summit was finally reached on 29 May 1953 and the news reached London on 2 June, just in time to be a fitting tribute at the Coronation of Queen Elizabeth II. Many young, up-and-coming climbers all over the world must have felt a pang of sorrow at their erstwhile greatest challenge having been removed.

Yet many exciting challenges still remain and not the least of them are to be found in rock climbing. Moreover, this is a sport that is within the reach of nearly everyone, since there are few parts of the world which do not possess outcrops of rocks or craggy coastlines. And it is often much harder and more hazardous to scale a 200-foot rock face than it is to climb a 10,000-foot moun-

Members of the expedition team.
Colonel John Hunt (centre), Sherpa
Tensing (left), Edmund Hillary (right)

tain. As a result, there are still several thousand rocks waiting to be attacked in Britain (where rock climbing is becoming almost a mania), whilst less than one per cent of potential climbs in the United States have so far been attempted.

As a sport, rock climbing is much older than mountaineering. The Romans regarded it as a healthy sport and there is evidence that the Emperor Hadrian scrambled up the escarpments of Mount Etna in 104 AD. We are told that Petrach frequently climbed in Provence in the fourteenth century. Also in France a monastery in the valley of the Dordogne established a climbing school as far back as 1426.

Rock climbing boasts two 'fathers', separated by some 325 years. The first was a certain Jean de Beaupré, who was appointed 'climbing instructor' to the court of Charles VIII of France in 1495. The second was an English Lake District shepherd, John Atkinson. In order to be able to rescue lost sheep on the mountains, he devised a method of rock climbing in 1825 and instructed others in the art. Even to this day climbers in the Lake District are frequently admonished with the words: 'That's no how auld Atkinson woulda done it.'

As we have seen, climbing has its historical background, but a lot more history is still in the making. After you have read this book, perhaps you may feel inclined to go out and add your own contribution to that history. On the other hand you may just be content with your own individual climbing for leisure.

2 THE MAKING OF A CLIMBER

Physical strength is not so important in a climber as determination and a clear head. In any event, strength can always be acquired to some degree, whereas the other two qualities are innate. However, it should be borne in mind that some people are temperamentally unsuited to climbing, just as some do not possess the right temperament to become good drivers. Climbing can bring out the worst in a man or woman besides the best. And, like yachting, it tests friendships to breaking point and soon separates the sheep from the goats.

Fortunately a large proportion of those who will never make good climbers lose their inclination to try as they grow older. Heights begin to bother them and the very thought of scaling a rock face or a mountain fills them with fear. Nevertheless there are still a few who insist upon having a go—usually as the result of vanity or bravado—and these are the people who are largely responsible for accidents.

The qualifications needed by the would-be climber are few in number, yet each is essential. In the first place, you need to be sound in wind and limb. If running up a steep flight of stairs makes your legs ache or leaves you gasping for breath, you may well be a non-starter. Secondly, you should not be subject to vertigo. The dizziness experienced when looking down at the ground from a considerable height can often be overcome, but if it persists you had better restrict your climbing activities to hill walking. Thirdly, you need a good sense of balance. If you are proficient at cycling, horsemanship or skiing, you are most likely well endowed with this quality already. If not, there are ways and means of acquiring it. Fourthly, you must be prepared to rough it. People who enjoy and demand their creature comforts at all times are seldom able to accustom themselves to the rigours of climbing. Finally, there is this matter of temperament, with which can be allied clearheadedness. Don't take up climbing if you are unable to make quick, sensible decisions or if you are inclined to panic when faced with the unexpected. The same thing applies if you are cursed with a hasty temper or do not possess a keen sense of humour. In other words, the born climber has exactly the same temperamental qualities as the born leader.

At what age should you begin climbing? I myself got to the top of my first high Alpine peak when I was just over ten. On the other hand, one of my closest mountaineering companions never set foot on a rock face until he was forty-three. So, within certain limits, age doesn't really matter, though most of today's great climbers took up the sport when they were at school.

Another question frequently asked is whether girls and women should go climbing. My answer to this is: by all means. Two of the best climbers I know are female—one of them, when still in her teens, liked to go scrambling up rock faces on a sunny day clad in little more than a bikini! The other is now a tough, delightful middle-aged woman who is a fully-qualified mountain guide. And a lot of us are unlikely to forget Nea Morin, who led all-women teams up the Alps in the thirties, and the magnificent Loulou Boulaz, who could climb better than most men of her age.

In some respects, women climbers have advantages over men. They are inclined to be more sure-footed, less hasty and to have a better sense of balance. And at high altitudes they find it easier to withstand low temperatures. Conversely, their smaller hands do not offer them so good a grip and petite women often find it physically impossible to climb with a heavy rucksack. I have yet to know of a woman acting as leader when climbing with a mixed party.

Exercises

We have seen that balance is of great importance in a climber and I have said that a sense of it can be acquired. It is not, however, necessary to go to the extent of learning to walk the tight-rope! A few simple exercises will suffice.

Begin by placing on the floor a fairly long board not more than three inches wide. Now walk up and down this board for ten minutes or so, one foot in front of the other, learning to turn as you come to each end. The next stage is to raise the board off the floor by supporting it on two chairs, then continue with the walking exercises as before. Finally, take the board outside and, using trestles or stepladders, raise it gradually a foot at a time, still continuing with the exercises. To gain poise, go through the whole process again, this time balancing a fairly heavy article, such as a bucket or a large book, on top of your head. Do this daily for a couple of weeks and you will find that you have vastly improved not only your sense of balance but also your deportment. You can better these even further by replacing the board with a tree trunk or branch about six inches in diameter, making sure that this is fixed firmly.

If heights make you feel dizzy, try a bit of ladder climbing for a few weeks. Begin at six feet and gradually increase the height until you can confidently reach thirty feet or more without your knees trembling. Also make a practice of going up to the top of high buildings and looking down from a window. Take an interest in what is going on down below and you will almost certainly find your vertigo disappearing.

Even comparatively simple rock climbing demands the accurate deployment of hands and feet. Most essential are supple fingers and a good, strong grip. Piano-playing will produce the suppleness. If you can't do this, practice every day with a tennis ball, rolling it in the fingers of each hand for ten minutes at a time. Most sports shops stock special finger-strengtheners and they should also be able to sell you a device for improving your grip. Swimming is good for your feet, but barefoot exercises morning and evening are even better. Try picking pencils and other small articles off the floor with your toes—it is not as difficult as it sounds.

Some of the stock physical training exercises—such as press-ups—will help to tone your abdominal muscles, but it is more important still for you to acquire a good power-weight ratio. This means in effect that your body should never be heavier than the strength in your arms and legs can comfortably support. It is often easier to lose weight than gain strength. Your legs are, of course, designed to hold you upright for very long periods yet, ideally, they must be able to carry you up long, steep inclines or flights of two hundred steps or more without becoming fatigued. Similarly, there should be enough strength in your hands and arms to keep you suspended off the ground for as long as ten minutes. If you have access to a gymnasium, put in a little regular work on the trapeze and parallel bars. And, whatever you do, use stairs as much as you can and don't be tempted by elevators.

Road work is vital. Drag yourself away from that automobile and take to your feet whenever possible. If you are a town-dweller, you may find it difficult to get out into the countryside except at week-ends, but don't let that worry you. Tramping the hard surfaces of urban sidewalks, particularly in hot weather, will help to strengthen your leg and ankle muscles.

Bearing in mind how much you are going to rely upon your feet, make absolutely sure that you are using the right footwear, even long before you begin climbing. It is really appalling how many men and women today wear shoes that are entirely unsuitable and one cannot be surprised that they suffer from foot ailments later in life. The practice stems mainly from vanity, I suppose, but I should hasten to add that no would-be climber can afford such indulgence. His shoes should be of the 'sensible' kind, not too tightly fitting, particularly at the heel, yet giving plenty of ankle support. His toes should be allowed to spread in their natural walking position and the shoes should be made of leather, so as to allow the feet to 'breathe'. Women who aspire to be climbers must, I regret to say, avoid wearing high heels as much as possible, especially when walking any distance, but solid, half-length heels are permissible.

Food and drink

Diet must be carefully considered when training to be a climber. Fatty foods are not to be recommended and red meats should be eaten sparingly. Conversely, you can let yourself go on fish, salads and fresh fruit. Eggs are permitted in fair quantity, but you should be wary about consuming too much bread and butter. Bitter chocolate will do you no harm but, if you have a desperate yen for sweetstuffs, try and stick to barley sugar. This, incidentally, is a great favourite with many climbers since it allays thirst and hunger and provides a ready source of energy.

You must also be careful about what you drink and how much. People who are accustomed to a large daily intake of liquid usually become thirsty very quickly and thirst can be an absolute menace when you are trying to make your way up a rock face on a hot day. In like manner heavy drinkers (and I don't mean those who fancy alcoholic beverages only) are often inclined to sweat profusely, which is another nuisance, particularly if it affects your hands. So try and keep your total intake down to no more than a pint and a half a day and restrict it to milk, tea, coffee and fruit juices, with an occasional glass of beer or stout. On no account should you touch the hard stuff, except in an emergency.

Having touched on some of the practical aspects of training, let us now deal with the theoretical side.

There are two reasonably simple subjects in which you must become proficient before you go climbing or even hill walking—map reading and compass reading. In hilly and mountainous country, mists, low cloud, heavy rain and sometimes snow not infrequently present awkward hazards and, unless you are sure of your bearings, can land you in real trouble.

Maps

Climbers in Britain are fortunate in having any number of excellent detailed maps at their disposal, thanks to Ordnance Survey. It is best to get hold of large scale ones ($2\frac{1}{2}$ inches to the mile or approximately 1:25,000) since these are big enough to show all the footpaths and recognizable landmarks, but a standard 1-inch map will often suffice, although you may need a magnifying-glass to help you read it. Most of the main hill walking and climbing areas in the United States are covered by 1:24,000 scale maps and some notable districts, like the Yosemite Valley, are exceptionally well charted. The Alps are mapped in scales ranging from 1:25,000 to 1:100,000 and the best guide books are those published by the Swiss Alpine Club and by Vallot in France. Many of them give indications of the standard of climb, viz. F (*facile*), D (*difficile*) and ED (*extrêment difficile*).

British Ordnance Survey maps have the additional advantage of being marked with National Grid numbers, which enable you to pinpoint positions with the utmost accuracy. Apart from this all

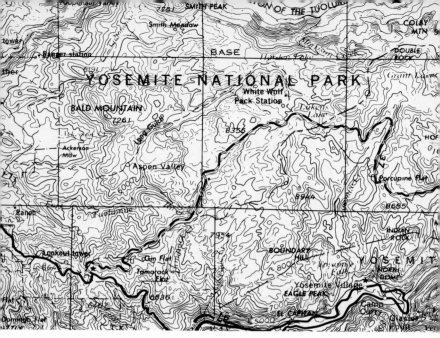

professional maps carry indications and markings that are standard in most of the countries where people climb for sport, though it is important for you to remember that distances and heights on European maps are marked in metres and kilometres and not in feet and miles (British maps should also be metric within the next few years.)

Contour lines are among the most important aids to the climber, for they not only give you some idea of the shape and size of a mountain but also indicate the steepness in gradients. The lines are brown in colour and are usually set at fifty-foot vertical intervals, meaning that there is a rise of fifty feet between each line. The actual heights above sea level are given at two hundred and fifty-foot intervals and the contour lines at these points are slightly thicker than the others. Some small-scale maps depict the heights of mountains by using different colours, but I should warn you that these are not a reliable guide.

Before you go climbing, you will find it an absorbing and profitable exercise to take paper, pencil and ruler and try to work out the vertical shape and height of a mountain from the information provided by the contour lines. When you've become expert in doing this, you'll be surprised how close your drawing will be to the real thing. Indeed, an artist of my acquaintance was able to paint several remarkably accurate pictures of Lake District peaks by using contour lines and without consulting references or moving one step from his London apartment!

You should also try and memorize as many as possible of the conventional signs used by mapmakers to indicate forests, spinneys, meadows, swamps, ponds, churches and so forth. This will save you from having to open up the whole map and search for the key when you want to take stock of your surroundings, a messy and difficult operation in a rainstorm or in the teeth of a strong wind.

A contour map showing the Yosemite
National Park in California USA

All good large-scale maps also give an indication of the magnetic variation, normally printed on the side borders. This is of vital importance to all seriously-minded hill walkers and climbers, as we shall now see.

Use of the compass
There are, as we all know, four Cardinal Points on every compass —North, South, East and West. But what may still be news to you is that there are actually two and sometimes three different Norths. These are True North, Magnetic North and, in the case of British maps only, Grid North. For the present, I shall confine myself to discussing the first two only.

Magnetic North is the point to which the needle of the compass is drawn and not, as one might expect, the site of the North Pole. The earth's *magnetic* pole lies in the north of Canada and varies its position slightly from year to year. Thus it will be appreciated that since the compass needle is attracted towards this position, it will never indicate True North (i.e. the North Pole) unless it is placed on the southward projection of a line joining these two Norths. Therefore there must otherwise always be a variation between the North shown on your compass and the North indicated on your map, either to the west or the east depending upon which part of the world you happen to be. The variation decreases or increases by one degree every six years and the current one in force is that given by your map, so you should be sure to have a map that is not out of date.

This brings us to the compass and the correct way to use it. You can buy a reasonably reliable compass for as little as a dollar in the United States, or fifty new pence in Britain, but I would strongly advise you to go the whole hog and obtain a really professional instrument. Nowadays a Scandinavian orienteering compass (see illustration p. 26) is always used.

As the name suggests, the figures on a prismatic compass are viewed through a prism, which is aligned with a hair line on the glass cover of the compass after it has been opened. Full instructions are always supplied with every instrument, so there is no need for me to detail them here. You must bear in mind, however, that the prismatic compass has one rather unfortunate disadvantage. If it is to be used for night climbing it has to be set in daylight and that might lead to an error in reading.

Although I have always advocated the use of a prismatic compass, I usually used a quite cheap little substitute on my own climbs. This is a liquid-filled model with a luminous dial, worn on the wrist and about the same size as a man's wristwatch. It was supplied to the British and American troops in the First World War and I bought it as an army surplus item in 1928 for five shillings. You can purchase one now for about five dollars, or two pounds sterling.

How to use the 'Silva' Compass:
1 Place the compass on your map with the left edge running from your present location to your destination

2 Rotate the compass until the North-South line is parallel with the vertical grid lines and North points to top of map

Finding True North (that is, the North to be found on all maps other than those publishing by Ordnance Survey) is comparatively simple. You read off the position of North given by your compass and then you add or subtract the magnetic variation, according to whether it is to the west or east. Thus if you want to travel on a bearing of 90 degrees as shown by your map (in other words, due East) and the magnetic variation is 10 degrees east, then you must set off on a bearing of 100 degrees as indicated on your compass. You will find this task very much easier still if you follow the diagram below.

On all O.S. maps you will find Grid North instead of or in addition to True North. This lies between True and Magnetic so you must be careful not to confuse the two variations when establishing

your bearings. Otherwise you might lose your way.

On a clear night another way of getting your bearings is by observing the stars. In the northern hemisphere this is extremely simple. The Pole Star never varies more than $2\frac{1}{2}$ degrees from True North and is easy enough to identify. Look first for the unmistakeable shape of the Great Dipper, also called the Great Bear (Ursa Major) and the Plough. This constellation consists of seven bright stars, arranged in the form of a saucepan with a bent handle. If you now draw an imaginary line through the two stars forming the side of the saucepan furthest from the handle, it will lead you straight to the Pole Star, readily distinguishable by its brilliance. Make a point of identifying the Pole Star every time you go out on

3 Lift compass off map and hold it horizontally until red end of compass needle points to N. The arrow will then show direction of travel

Magnetic North deflects the needle about 10° from True North. This difference should be added to your bearing
4 Illustration of compass

a starry night; it may be of great assistance to you later on.

There is one other thing you should do before you set out on your first hill walk. Decide first where you intend to go, then get your map of the district and buy or borrow as many books as you can describing the district. Armed with these, take a pencil and notebook and make a few maps of your own. It doesn't matter how crude they are as long as they indicate the routes you wish to take and give details of inclines and landmarks which will help you to keep on the right course. It is also a good idea to jot down the compass bearings you will encounter on your walk.

I always used to do this whenever I climbed in the Alps and I can assure you that I often found my sketch maps a great deal more helpful than the printed ones I carried.

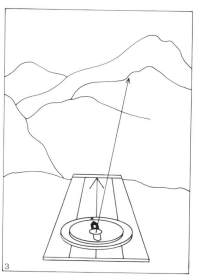
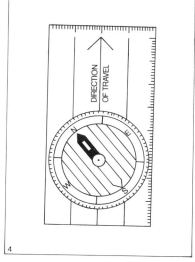

DIRECTION OF TRAVEL

Clothing and Equipment

Finally, a few words about the basic clothing and equipment you will need for hill walking. For the top part of your body an anorak is ideal and, if you really want to do yourself proud, buy yourself one of the quilted ones stuffed with down, which adds little to the weight and keeps you comfortably warm in the cold. Otherwise a medium weight, turtle-neck woollen sweater, loosely knit, will suffice, though it might be advisable to carry a spare under sweater as a precaution against drops in temperature. Two thin sweaters are usually warmer than one thick one.

Do **not** wear slacks or a skirt. The former, no matter how well they may fit, will hamper the free movement of your legs and pre-

A group of hill walkers pause for a rest.
For some hill walking is the first step on
the road to rock climbing. To others it
is a pleasant and invigorating pastime

vent you from seeing that your feet find the right holds. Skirts also obscure the feet and can actually be dangerous—not to speak of immodest!—when there are strong winds blowing. Short breeches, buckling just below the knee and preferably made of whipcord or stout tweed, are by far the best attire. Ideally they should be made with a double seat, with a piece of thin water-proofing material or leather between the two seats, so that you may sit down comfortably on rough or damp ground. For the lower legs wear thick woollen socks, reinforced at the toes and heels.

In really hot weather, shorts may be worn if preferred, the Bermuda type being best. But don't go about bare-kneed if you intend to do a bit of rock scrambling, since you are liable to scratch yourself badly.

The right sort of underwear is of major importance. For both men and women a string shirt is desirable, because it allows the free circulation of air at the same time keeping the body at a warm, even temperature. But string shirts have one unfortunate disadvantage. If you are carrying a heavy load on your back—as you may well have to do on a long-distance walk—you are liable to find the strings cutting into your back and shoulders. In such

cases, it is best to wear a thin woollen undervest, or even two in
cold weather. In the last few years there have been great im-
provements in underwear. 'Damart' underwear made from an
artificial pile is much warmer than string and wool shirts.

Never go hill walking without something on your head. In sunny
weather a broad-brimmed felt hat, or perhaps a Panama, will be
found very suitable, but it is advisable to take with you a balaclava
or a knitted ski cap in case it turns cold. A climbing helmet may
also be necessary in rocky places and you will find advice on how
to choose one in a later chapter.

Most important of all is, of course, footwear. Though some
people still like to go hill walking in stout shoes, I do not recom-
mend the practice. Good tough boots, lined with some soft
material such as fleece or sponge rubber, are the correct wear
and great care must be taken that they fit snugly without pressing
on or chafing any part of the foot. Unlike your everyday footwear,
they should have thick, moulded rubber soles if you are going to
cover wet ground and they should also be fairly flexible with as
wide a heel as possible. Above all, they need to be well stitched
and completely watertight.

Climbers must pay scrupulous attention to personal hygiene. It is often difficult to come across full washing facilities when hill walking in remote areas, so it is all the more essential that you should try to keep your body as clean as possible. All underwear must be changed daily, even if it does not appear to be soiled. Sweaters that have become affected by perspiration must be washed as soon as possible and socks should be frequently rinsed and carefully dried before re-use. At the end of a day's walk, boots must be thoroughly cleaned, then completely unlaced and left in a warm place to air, with their tongues pulled down to expose the interior.

During the course of a walk, remove your boots whenever you halt for a rest and shake them well in case any grit has managed to get inside. Then take off your socks and examine your feet. If you find any signs of chafing deal with them immediately, using strips of 'breathable' surgical plaster rather than ointment. If there is a mountain stream nearby, it is often a good plan to dip your feet into it for two or three minutes, but make sure they are quite dry before putting on your socks again.

On a hot day you are almost certain to be affected by sunburn, even at comparatively low altitudes, so you should always carry and use one of the reputable makes of sun-tan lotion or ointment sold by drug stores. Insects, too can be a nuisance at certain times of the year, but you can stave off their attacks by dabbing a little oil of geranium or oil of verbena on your hands and face.

The basic equipment you will require will increase in size and quantity as you graduate through hill walking to rock climbing and eventually to true mountaineering, so I will deal with it at intervals throughout this book, just as I will also mention camping equipment in a later chapter. Primarily for hill walking you will require your compass, your maps, a stout walking-stick with a pointed steel ferrule, a good rucksack or knapsack with or without a frame and, of course, a reliable watch. A few simple cooking utensils, together with the necessary butane- or propane-operated miniature cooker and a supply of foodstuffs, must be carried on a long walk, and you should not forget to include a small first-aid case, a powerful whistle and a good electric torch (which should incorporate a flashing device) in case of emergencies. A full water-bottle is a 'must', though you should try and use its contents sparingly, and you may find it advisable to take with you a pair of anti-glare spectacles, preferably of the polarized type. If you are expecting to encounter any steep climbs, it would be a good idea to take a 30-foot coil of climbing rope along with you, but I'll deal with ropes in more detail when we come to rock climbing.

One last hint. Make sure that the anorak or sweater you are going to wear is brightly-colored or carries a large color patch. This will enable you to be more easily spotted by a rescue party if you injure yourself or run into difficulties.

3 HILL CLIMBING

Talk to any experienced mountaineer and you will almost certainly discover that he learnt his art progressively. He started by making excursions into the hills, then he had a spell of rock climbing, beginning with simple ascents and gradually progressing to slow, arduous struggles up steep faces, before he considered himself proficient enough to tackle the high peaks.

This is the only correct procedure. You will never be a safe, competent climber until you have attuned your body—and your head—to all the strains that really hard mountaineering can impose and all the hazards you may encounter on your way. And you should begin with the hills, for there is much elementary knowledge to be acquired on their slopes.

Hill climbing for pleasure is more frequently referred to as fell walking. This is because, as I mention in the first chapter, the sport originated in the fells of the English Lake District. It was, in fact, a Lakeland shepherd who first led parties of tourists across the fells in the mid-nineteenth century and, ever since then, the Lake District has attracted enthusiastic climbers from all parts of the world and has become one of the accepted 'nurseries' and training grounds for mountaineers. Edward Whymper learnt his techniques here, so did many of the members of the victorious Mount Everest expedition. Even so, there are plenty of other places where you can gain a like experience and I suggest you study your maps, find the nearest locality that offers steep rises up to eight hundred feet or more and make your start there.

Before you set out, make a short list of all the equipment you should take with you and check each item as you stow it away in your knapsack. You may consider this an unnecessary reminder, yet you would be surprised to know how many fell walkers forget to take this very simple precaution and land themselves in difficulties as a result. Your list should read as follows:

Large-scale map of area
Guide book to area (if available)
Compass
Protractor
Electric torch (Flashlight) with spare battery
Whistle on lanyard
Pocket knife with 3 or 4 blades
Small first aid box
Sandwiches (cheese or meat filling, but nothing salty or savoury)
Bar of plain chocolate
Packet of barley sugar
Packet of mints
Vacuum flask (filled with hot tea, coffee or milk)
One light, woollen mixture sweater
One pair of clean socks
Two clean handkerchiefs
Sun tan lotion or cream

Of course, some of these items may be carried in your pockets, but you should remember that there is always a risk of them falling out and getting lost. And, finally, don't forget to wear your watch and make sure it is showing the right time.

General hints
As soon as you start your climb, set your pace firmly and try to stick to it for the whole of the journey. Whatever you do, don't walk fast and don't take long strides. The recognized 'guide's pace' of between 70 and 80 steps a minute is by far the best to adopt, both on the flat and on inclines. If you walk with one foot about six inches in front of the toe of the other, this pace will carry you forward at the rate of two miles an hour. This may at first appear much too slow and you will probably get a bit impatient, but you should be able to cover at least twenty miles in this manner without feeling overtired.

Body posture is also of prime importance. Walking straight-backed military fashion may be right for the parade ground, but it is quite senseless when climbing. Your aim should be to achieve perfect balance at all times and on all gradients. Throw the weight of your body forward when ascending and backward when descending, at the same time flexing your knees. Use the balls of your toes when going uphill and the flats of your heels on downhill stretches.

You will soon discover that, in climbing, the shortest distance is not necessarily a straight line between two points. In terms of measurement this may be so but in terms of time it often is not. When tackling a steep gradient it is always best to take a zig-zag course, which will enable you to maintain your steady pace and still have plenty of breath left after completing the ascent. Where marked paths exist—as is usually the case in popular climbing terrain—be sure to keep to them, otherwise you may find yourself

treading on dangerous ground or floundering in some bog. Do
not attempt to take short cuts; they often lead you into trouble and
you may well get lost.

I have dwelt on the need for well-fitting boots and your first
climb should prove whether you have chosen wisely. If you begin
to feel any symptoms of chafing, don't try to grin and bear it.
Remove your boots and socks, place a thin strip of cushioned
plaster over the chafed skin, then see whether you can discover
the cause of the trouble and remedy it. You may find it a good plan
to slip on an extra pair of socks before replacing your boots.
Don't pull them the whole way up your legs, since this is likely to
cause overheating, but roll them down neatly over the tops of the
boots. If the chafing still persists, it will be much better to cut
short your climb rather than end up with an agonizing blister.

In the past I have found it useful to add an extra pair of boots to
my check list. These should be slightly looser fitting than the ones
you normally wear so that, by changing into them, you will be
able to relieve any tightness or chafing you may experience.

Most fell walking routes in the Lake
District are clearly marked by little
piles of stones at quarter mile intervals.
These are known as cairns

A short rest is advizable after each hour of walking, but it should
never be of more than ten minutes' duration, otherwise muscular
stiffness may set in. If you have been climbing in strong sunlight,
choose a resting place that is sheltered from the sun's rays.
Then, after you have sat down, remove your boots, loosen your
clothing and relax. Some climbers like to have a smoke during
their rest period, but I am not in favour of this. In my humble
opinion, smoking and climbing simply don't mix. Your lungs need
all the fresh air they can accommodate and even a single cigar-
ette can affect your breathing.

On the other hand, a rest will afford you a good opportunity to
take in some nourishment and a little food and drink will help to
replace the energy you have expended. But be sure that it *is* a
little, for if you gorge yourself on all the provisions you have
brought along, you will be too satiated to be in a fit condition to
continue your climb. It is much better to take small amounts of
food at frequent intervals rather than to consume the lot at one
go. Drink from your vacuum flask and don't be tempted by any
sparkling streams you may encounter. In the first place you can
never be sure that the water is not contaminated, no matter how
crystal clear it may appear. Secondly, most mountain and hill
spring water is extremely cold and drinking it can give you
stomach cramps and sometimes diarrhoea.

Try and restrict your first climbs to the hours of daylight.
Climbing in the dark can often be hazardous, particularly if you
are not well acquainted with the route. If you have planned a climb
carefully with the aid of your map, you will have been able to cal-
culate approximately how long it will take you to complete and it
is a good idea to add another couple of hours for contingencies.
Thus, if you are proposing to embark on a fell walk covering
12 miles, allow 6 hours for actual walking, another hour for resting
and 2 hours contingency time, making 9 hours in all. If the period
between sunrise and sunset is less than this, take a shorter walk.

Even so, unforeseen difficulties, such as losing your way in a

mist, may result in your being benighted. If this is the case, you should proceed with extreme care. You should never panic and try to increase your speed; instead you should shorten your pace and cut the rate down to 20 or 30 a minute. Now is when your electric torch (flashlight) will come in handy, but you must use it sparingly. Shine it ahead for two or three minutes, so that you and your party can see what lies in front of you and be able to identify any hazards in the path, such as projecting boulders or roots. Then switch off the light, wait until your eyes have become re-accustomed to the darkness, and proceed cautiously over the ground that you illuminated. Continue in this manner and your torch (flashlight) is not likely to fail you, though you may have to use your spare battery. It is doubtful whether you will have a rope with you—fell walkers don't usually carry them—so, if you feel apprehensive, particularly when descending a steep gradient, keep very close together in Indian file, so that those following the leader can always grab the man in front if any difficulty arises. It is sometimes a good idea, when negotiating exceptionally rough ground, to link hands and walk sideways.

Weather
Mist or low cloud at night presents a special problem, because it is often impossible to see more than a few feet ahead and the beam of your torch usually does more harm than good. If you should feel at all apprehensive of carrying on in such conditions, the only sensible thing to do is to stay where you are and wait until daylight. Unless the weather is bitterly cold, this should prove quite an easy matter, and the more people in the party the better it will be. Endeavour to find a spot where the ground is reasonably dry and sheltered from air currents, such as a clearing between two boulders or among trees, then put on what extra garments you may have brought with you and huddle up closely together. The main essential is to keep as warm and dry as possible and five or six people between them can generate a great deal more heat than two. You may light a fire if you have the necessary materials handy, but this presents certain disadvantages. It may refuse to burn properly, in which case it will emit more irritating fumes than heat, and it will almost certainly require constant tending. The coldest period usually sets in about two hours before the dawn and, if you find the chill too severe, rouse yourself and your companions, make them take off their extra clothing and spend from a quarter to half an hour doing physical exercises before replacing the garments and settling down again. You will be surprised how much warmer you will feel.

Mist is only one of the difficulties you are liable to encounter when fell walking, so perhaps we had better discuss some of the other hazards in more detail.

Bad weather has always been and will always be the climber's

Winter weather conditions can often present a fell walker with difficult and dangerous ground. This is on the northern slopes of the Cairngorm Range in Scotland.

greatest enemy. There is a very obvious reason for this, since it is in hilly and mountainous areas that weather conditions are most likely to change suddenly without any warning. You can begin a climb on what appears to be a glorious sunny day without a cloud in the sky, only to be engulfed a few hours later in mist, driving rain or even a blizzard. Thunderstorms also blow up very quickly in the mountains. Although most of them don't last very long, they can often be very unnerving.

Your best plan, of course, is to try and avoid climbing whenever the conditions seem uncertain, but I know of very few climbers who are reasonably good weather prophets and meteorology is far too complicated a science for most of us to grasp with any degree of proficiency. Even the experts frequently come unstuck when forecasting the weather in regions that are well above sea level. So when in doubt don't climb.

Cloud formations
1 **Cirrus** usually denotes fine weather
2 **Cirrostratus** means rain within 24 hours
3 **Cumulus** means fair weather
4 **Nimbus** with Cumulus forms Cumulonimbus

5 **Cumulonimbus** which indicates approaching rain
6 **Stratus** usually indicates dense mist at heights of 500 feet or more

At the same time, you can learn quite a lot by studying cloud formations. They will at least tell you when high winds, heavy rains and snowstorms are to be expected. Some of the commonest types of cloud formation are illustrated opposite. **Cirrus** (**1**) will be seen as delicate, feathery clouds through which the sun is able to shine and these usually denote fine weather unless they come together to form **Cirrostratus** (**2**) which is indicative of rain within 24 hours. **Cumulus** (**3**) is also a fair weather formation until it joins with **Nimbus** (**4**) to form **Cumulonimbus** (**5**) a sure sign of approaching heavy rain or hail. Nimbus itself is a formation of dark, threatening clouds and predicts continuous rain or snow. Most important from the mountaineer's point of view is **Stratus** (**6**), since this is low altitude cloud and the main cause of dense mist at heights of 500 feet and more.

You have been told what to do should mist descend during the hours of darkness, but it also vitally important to know what course to take when you encounter mist in daytime. First and foremost, you must establish your position the moment you observe mist approaching and before it blots out visibility. Use your map and compass to do this and then examine your map carefully to see whether there are any emergency descents in the near vicinity. If there are, they will enable you to lose altitude quickly and so escape the descending cloud. In any case, if the mist is heavy, your objective should be to take a downward path and to avoid climbing any higher if you possibly can. Whatever happens, do not proceed any further if the track is not clearly defined; the prudent thing to do in that case is to return whence you came. On the other hand, you might be caught by the mist when not following a clearly marked path, in which case you will have to resort to your compass. When taking such a course, it is imperative that you take a careful note of all prominent features you encounter en route. This will enable you to find your way back if you come to a dead end.

Heavy falls of rain or sleet can be just as disconcerting as mist, reducing visibility almost to nil. If you feel that these conditions are not likely to abate and there is no sense in sheltering, you should take the same precautions as you do for mist. However, when you run into a thunderstorm, it is highly advizable for you to take shelter at once, especially if the lightning is close at hand, but on no account go and stand under a tree as you may be struck. Unfortunately the best thing in thunder is to sit huddled up away from trees, large boulders or water courses but this usually means you cannot shelter.

If you are new to fell walking, do please resist the temptation to leave the path and indulge in a sport of rock climbing. In the course of my experience, I have come across innumerable cases where eager but foolhardy amateurs have scrambled up crags only to find themselves stranded in a position from which they can neither descend nor ascend. Mountaineers describe this predicament as being 'cragfast' and have laid down certain rules of procedure for climbers who become stuck in this manner. If you should ever suffer such an unfortunate experience, remember that you must not panic. Stay where you are, making yourself as secure as possible, then take out your whistle and blow an SOS on it at regular intervals. This consists of three short, three long and three short blasts (··· ——— ···). It is almost certain that your call will be heard by somebody, but don't be alarmed if help doesn't come for several hours. If night falls, alternate your whistle signals with three short, three long and three short flashes on your torch, providing visibility is good. There is also another recognized code—six blasts on a whistle or six flashes on a torch for help.

Whilst on the subject of whistling, I must warn you never to use your whistle except in emergency, no matter what sort of blasts you blow upon it. I have known two cases where a Mountain Rescue Team has been called out simply because a climber had been blowing a whistle just for fun. Another 'crime' is to indulge in the childish habit of sliding or throwing stones over precipices. You should remember that even one small stone coming in contact with others on its downward path is capable of starting a dangerous avalanche.

Clothing and equipment

When you have acquired sufficient experience in summer fell walking, you may consider yourself fit enough to tackle the same climbs in the winter. This will bring you in contact with snow and ice and thus equip you with some of the skills you will require before you graduate to alpinism. You will, of course, need to make some changes in your attire. A padded anorak is essential as is a woollen cap or Balaclava, and you should buy yourself some waterproof and windproof overtrousers, such as cyclists wear in bad weather. You must also wear thick woollen gloves and, in very cold weather, have a pair of woollen mittens beneath and a waterproof overpair on top. Domestic rubber gloves will serve in good stead if you can't obtain the real thing. Finally you should wear two or even three pairs of woollen socks and two thick pullovers (with two spares in your knapsack). Otherwise you will get very cold. You can still retain your rubber-soled boots even in very icy conditions.

It is advisable to carry with you a pair of ice-climbing crampons to attach to your boots but, even if you don't do this, it is imperative to equip yourself with an ice axe. This should be between two and a half and three feet in length (the standard Alpine axe is 1 metre) with a head consisting of a pick 6–7 inches long and a flat or curved blade 4 inches long tapering from a width of 3 inches. The axe should, of course, be fitted with a spiked ferrule.

Use of the ice axe

I always consider that the word axe is a bit of a misnomer, for there are so many different things you can do with this useful tool once you have learnt to handle it properly. Indeed, one can say in all truth that but for the ice axe climbers would be in a very sorry state. Many lives have depended on it in the past and few high mountains could ever have been climbed without its assistance.

First you must learn how to carry your axe correctly, otherwise you may find it more of a hindrance than a help. If you do not envisage using it during the early part of your climb, you should pack it inside your rucksack to prevent it catching on things. Always remember that the ferrule must be uppermost. Otherwise carry it as you would a sporting gun, with the head tucked under your left armpit (right armpit if you are left-handed) and the ferrule pointed at an angle of forty-five degrees towards the ground. It is a good idea to protect the axe edge, pick point and ferrule with rubber or leather guards and in certain countries, such as France and Switzerland, this is legally compulsory on trains and other forms of public transport.

The ice axe makes an effective brake if you ever find yourself sliding down an ice or snow slope. In fact, whenever you tackle one of these slopes you should have the axe ready to use immediately. The illustrations show the two best methods of braking. You can either lie lengthwise along the shaft and use both hands to drive the pick into the slippery surface or you can grasp the lower part of the shaft with one hand, drive the pick into the ground with the other and wedge the axe blade under your armpit. Don't forget that, in order to get as good and deep a 'bite' as possible with your pick, you must use as much body weight as you can upon it.

Perfect braking can only come with plenty of practice. So, when you go winter fell walking, find a convenient ice slope that is not too steep and too long and spend several hours on it, sliding down it again and again until you feel confident you can arrest your slide at any given point. When I used to climb in the Alps every summer and winter I used to spend my first day in the mountains practising sliding and braking and I have reason to be eternally grateful for taking this precaution.

Sliding need not necessarily be dangerous unless it is accidental; it can be used to considerable advantage when making rapid descents, providing it is properly controlled. This technique is known as **glissading** and, once you have mastered the art of braking, you will find that controlled sliding is both helpful and exhilarating. But I must warn you never to attempt it unless you have previously examined the slope (probably on your way up) and found it to be firm and negotiable, otherwise you could well find yourself involved with an avalanche.

An ice axe comes in particularly handy when you are walking
side on to a steep slope. Don't use it as you would a walking-stick,
but aim the ferrule higher up the slope—at a point that is approximately level with your knees—and use it to keep yourself vertical.
This will enable you to keep both feet firmly on the ground and
thus get the best possible grip.

Mountain rescue

In nearly all the recognized fell walking districts in the world you
will find highly trained Mountain Rescue teams. They are there
to render immediate assistance if you or any member of your
climbing party becomes a casualty and is so badly ill or injured or
so far away from base that he cannot be helped by his companions.

It is essential, before you go on any climb, that you should know
the exact location of the nearest Mountain Rescue headquarters.
You will probably find it marked on your map but, if you are in any
doubt, make enquiries in one of the towns or villages in the area
you are intending to explore. Also ascertain the quickest ways to
the headquarters from any point along the route you propose to
traverse. If an emergency should occur—and I sincerely hope
that it never will—you or one of your party should set off at once
taking with you or him the following details: (a) a large-scale map
showing exactly where the casualty may be found; (b) a brief
description of any outstanding landmarks in the vicinity, to enable
the rescuers to pinpoint the spot visually; and (c) a description of
the casualty's injuries or illness, so that the appropriate medical
equipment and supplies may be conveyed to him. Whenever
possible, you should try to assist the rescuers by marking the
casualty's whereabouts in some manner, such as making flags
with sticks and handkerchiefs.

Mountain rescue teams are dedicated men and women who
usually work on a purely voluntary basis (except in certain Alpine
areas), so they should never be called out unless it is strictly
necessary. On the other hand, they must be alerted at once if you
believe a casualty's injuries to be serious and at all times when a
casualty has suffered a severe fall. If their headquarters are at
some distance from the scene of the accident, remember that
they can always be contacted from any dwelling that has a tele-
phone or from any public call box. All you have to do is to ask for
the operator and you will be put straight through.

In conclusion, let me stress once again that many mountain
tragedies could be averted if every climbing party only made sure
of informing others of their intentions. Before you start out, tell
the management of your hotel exactly where you are going to
climb and at what time you may be expected back. If you are not
staying at an hotel, inform the local police or get in touch with the
Mountain Rescue people. No one will consider this a nuisance. On
the contrary, they will respect you for it.

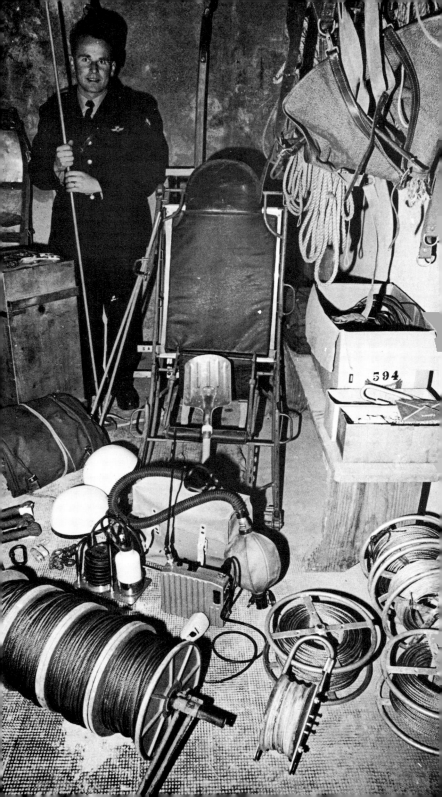

4 ROCK CLIMBING

Your experiences in fell walking will by now have taught you most of the basic principles of climbing and will have convinced you one way or the other whether you are a fit enough person to be let loose on the rocks. If you lack tenacity, get tired quickly or suffer from vertigo in precipitous places, then let me advise you straight away to steer clear of rock climbing. At the same time, these deficiencies should not prevent you from going on some of the easier Alpine climbs, so do not lose heart but just turn right away to Chapter 5.

Rocks are among Mother Nature's greatest deceivers. A grim, towering crag that appears at first sight to be completely insurmountable may turn out to be as easy to climb as a stepladder, whilst an insignificant looking rock no bigger than a giant boulder may often defeat the most experienced mountaineer. I can recall one climb in particular that aggravated me beyond belief for a number of years. It is a rock not much more than fifty feet high, situated near Tunbridge Wells in Southern England, and it looks as innocent as a new-born babe. Yet it has defeated nine out of every ten climbers who have tried to reach its puny summit.

Types of rock
Many times I have heard it said and seen it written that a climber can never judge how difficult a rock may be until he has rubbed noses with it. I would go even further than that and contend that no one should attempt even the easiest of rock climbs unless he has a fairly good grasp of rock structure in general. I therefore strongly advise all aspirants to study one or two simple books on the subject before starting to climb but, in the meantime, I will deal very briefly with some of the commonest types of rock you are likely to encounter in almost every part of the world.

In my humble opinion **gritstone** is certainly the best rock on which to learn to climb. It is in fact coarse sandstone, frequently blackened by the addition of carboniferous particles, and was once the source of most millstones. From the climber's point of view it is ideal since, although mostly steep, it presents a good friction surface and, as the illustration overleaf (**1**) shows, offers plenty of footholds. Gritstone is usually found in coal mining areas, forming outcrops that may rise to two hundred feet or more.

Crystalline rocks, such as gneiss and granite (**5**), are almost entirely restricted to mountain areas and, whilst often offering little in the way of holds, are popular with climbers because of their firmness. Another crystalline, **dolomite** (**2**), can sometimes prove treacherous, since its projections have a nasty habit of breaking away suddenly. **Basalt** (**4**), which is an igneous rock, should also be avoided by inexperienced climbers because of its looseness, which is particularly pronounced after heavy rainfalls. It may easily be distinguished by its colour, which is black, glossy and not unlike coal in its appearance.

Learning rock climbing on the 'Long Layback Harrison's Rock in the south of England

Sandstone (3) appears more frequently than any other rock and outcrops of it may often be found within a short distance of many towns and cities. Like gritstone it offers a good climbing surface, but you should bear in mind that it is of a comparatively soft nature and should be scaled with care.

General hints
There are three golden rules that the rock climbing beginner must always obey. Firstly, never attempt to climb any rock that has not been safely climbed before by many others with similar lack of experience. Secondly, always make sure that the holds you use when climbing will also permit you to make a safe descent. Thirdly, never give way to panic and don't consider it beneath your dignity to call for help should you run into any difficulty and

Typical rock formations
1 Gritstone
2 Dolomite
3 Sandstone
4 Basalt
5 Granite

3

5

find yourself cragfast. To these I would like to add a rule of my own: never go rock climbing on your own and without at least one experienced climber as a companion.

There are two distinct kinds of rock climbing—free and artificial. In the former, you rely solely upon the aids that God gave you, namely your hands and feet. This does not mean to say that you will not carry a rope and other artificial aids with you, for you may need these if you run into difficulty. On the other hand, you should have ample experience of free climbing before you graduate to climbs that demand the use of these aids. If you have a climbing school somewhere in your vicinity, do try and make use of it. It is infinitely better to learn the fundamentals from a thoroughly qualified instructor and the fees will not be expensive.

Clothing and equipment
You will have to make modifications to your clothing before venturing on the rocks. Choosing the right underwear is a very important consideration, because you will find yourself sweating much more than you did when fell walking. Years ago, when I first started climbing seriously, I used to favour vests (undershirts) and long underpants made entirely of wool, but I soon discovered these tended to cause heat rashes and I wisely changed to string garments, which not only allowed the sweat to evaporate quickly but, surprisingly enough, kept me warmer. Many male climbers now wear these, though it is sometimes difficult to persuade a fastidious female to adopt them!

Slacks are not to be recommended, as they are liable to cause discomfort and may even prove hazardous at times. Knee-breeches are the order of the day, since they permit more freedom of movement and can be unfastened at the knee when the weather is warm. Make sure they are made of some strong material resistant to abrasion, such as Bedford cord, cavalry twill or heavy tweed. It is best to support them with braces (known as suspenders in the United States) and this applies equally to both men and women. On no account use a belt, since this will interfere with the adjustment of your rope waist loop. Make sure that the breeches fit comfortably and that they are reinforced at the seat and at the knees, preferably with a double layer of material. Long, all-woollen socks should be worn with them, extending as far as the knee-cap, so that the breeches will overlap them by about two inches. On no account should any bare skin be exposed or you will soon find yourself suffering from scratches and bruises.

You can wear almost any kind of shirt you prefer, so long as it is not made of man-made fibre. A light flannel shirt is ideal in the summer, but I always opt for a coarse woollen lumberjack shirt in colder weather or when climbing at high altitudes. Over this you should wear a sweater, but be sure it is not too heavy or so loosely woven that it can catch on projections on the rock face.

The anorak you wore when fell walking is perfectly suitable for rock climbing, though you should make sure that it is loose-fitting enough to allow full freedom of movement. Another type of outer garment that is gaining popularity, particularly with mountaineers, is the *cagoule*. This is a sort of smock made in polyurethane which comes down to just below your knees and weighs little more than eight ounces. The *cagoule* can be very valuable if you ever have the misfortune to be caught in a storm or get stranded overnight. You have only to squat down and it will form a protective tent.

Footwear is largely a matter of choice and here you should always seek the advice of an expert, because boots that are suitable for one type of rock may be quite unsuitable or even dangerous for another type. In any case, I would strongly advise you to invest in a pair of PA's. These are canvas-topped boots with smooth composition soles and they give you a really excellent grip. They owe their abbreviated name to their inventor, the famous French guide Pierre Allain.

Most rock climbers refrain from wearing gloves, since they interfere with hand holds, but this should not deter you from carrying a pair for use in emergencies. On occasions when you have to let a rope slip through your hands they will protect you from burns. In icy conditions, when your fingers are likely to become numbed, it is permissible to wear thin silk or nylon gloves. Those worn by surgeons will be found ideal. Mittens are also helpful.

Finally, you will need a safety helmet. Do not for one moment imagine there is anything 'sissy' about wearing such headgear. On the contrary, any fully fledged climber will tell you that the helmet is quite the most sensible piece of attire that has ever been devised since, before its introduction, nearly fifty per cent of all climbing accidents involved serious head injuries, caused either by falls or by falling stones. But you must remember that a climbing helmet is specially designed for the job and is not the same as those worn by motorcyclists or workers on building sites. In the first place, it has to be made as light as possible without sacrificing any degree of strength and this entails the use of special plastics. Secondly, it must be well ventilated, as there is nothing that can irritate a climber more than beads of sweat pouring down from his head and blinding his eyes. Thirdly, the helmet must be so designed as not to obstruct vision or hearing and, lastly, it must have a secure, foolproof fastening so that it won't fall off should you have the misfortune to fall yourself. A good helmet should never weigh more than 18 ounces and, whatever you do, don't try to save by buying an inferior make.

I should emphasize here that you will not need your helmet on every climb. On simple ascents, where there is little danger of falling and where there are few loose stones, the only headgear required is a wollen cap or a Balaclava.

As you progress with your rock climbing you will find it necessary to acquire quite a lot of new, specialized equipment and, since some of the items are bound to be expensive, it will be best to buy the various items in dribs and drabs, as and when required. But the first and most important essential is a good rope. Here, once again, you should never buy cheaply, because a climber's life can so easily depend solely upon the quality of the rope he uses.

Rope

Until twenty-five years ago, all climbing ropes were made of either hemp or manilla, although some of the earlier mountaineers used to pin their faith in silken ropes, which were tremendously strong but also extremely costly. Hempen ropes are still favoured by a few veteran climbers but, since the evolution of synthetic fibres, the nylon rope has virtually replaced the more orthodox types because of its lightness, elasticity and high tensile strength. It is still not as strong as pure silk but it is nearly twice as strong as hemp or manilla. Nylon also has the advantages of being rotproof, impervious to wet and unaffected by freezing. Conversely, it weakens and may even melt if it is subjected to high temperatures or excessive friction but, as it is possible to guard against such conditions, this disadvantage need not be regarded too seriously.

Climbing ropes are usually of two types—the hawser and the *kernmantel*. In the former the fibres are twisted together, and in the latter the rope consists of a core of fibres enclosed in an outer nylon sheath which is added for protective purposes. In making your choice of which type to use you should bear in mind the following facts. The *kernmantel* is slightly stronger than the hawser by weight/strength ratio, but it has a tendency to kink and an extension of little more than 25 per cent. The hawser, on the other hand, is more pliable and has an extension of from 40 per cent to 50 per cent.

This business of extension is of vital importance, because the longer a rope will extend under a sudden shock load the less likely it is to snap. It is for this reason that I would advise you to plump for a hawser.

You still have to make a choice as to the size of rope you require, although you may decide to go the whole hog and select one example of each of the four sizes most generally available. The smallest, No. 1 size has a diameter of one-seventh of an inch, weighs 20 ounces per 100 feet and has a minimum breaking load of 1,000 lb. The specification then progresses as follows: No. 2 one-fifth, 40, 2,000; No. 3 two-fifths, 68, 3,500; No. 4 five-twelfths, 88, 4,200. The No. 3 or No. 4 are those always used today.

Some of my climbing friends seem set against using nylon as a waistline, since there is some likelihood of it weakening due to

Left: In the *hawser* the fibres are twisted, whilst in the *kernmantel*. Right: they are enclosed in a sheath

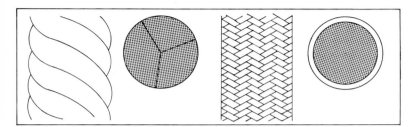

frictional heat, and prefer a hempen rope for this purpose. Having never yet experienced any trouble of this nature I am not wholly convinced as to the value of this precaution, but it is nevertheless a point that should always be borne in mind.

Whatever type of rope you decide upon, you must remember to maintain it with loving care. Check it thoroughly after each climb, examine it at regular intervals, store it in a cool, dry place and keep it well away from any substance that might possibly corrode it. If you detect any flaw or the slightest sign of wear or fraying in your rope, scrap it at once and buy a new one. Never forget it's not just a rope, it's a lifeline.

Some climbing manoeuvres necessitate the use of double roping. In such cases it is a good idea to dye one of the ropes red or green to distinguish it from the other. Don't do the dyeing yourself, in case you use the wrong materials and corrode or weaken the rope, but entrust it to a ropemaker. Many ropemakers supply ropes already coloured.

The nylon rope has one further disadvantage in that it cannot be knotted so effectively as hemp or manilla. The fibre is of such a slippery nature that some of the more conventional knots are not to be trusted and, indeed, new knotting techniques have had to be devised in order to cope with the new situation.

Knots

You *must* know your knots before you go climbing. There are at least six you have to master and when I say master I mean that you should be able to tie them instinctively under all kinds of conditions—in the dark, with one hand only and even when your

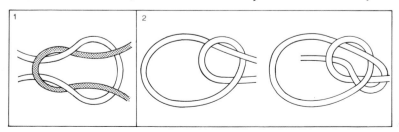

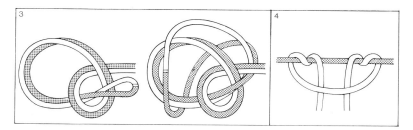

fingers are paralysed with cold. On the efficiency of one single, simple knot may depend the safety not only of yourself but of all those who are climbing with you.

Learn to tie two knots first; the **reef knot** (1), which is the simplest of all but which so often can result in a dangerous 'granny' and the **bowline**, an all-purpose knot that has so often got so many people out of difficulties (2). A simple method of learning the bowline technique is to think of a rabbit coming out of its hole, taking a quick look round and then going back again. You fashion the hole by making a loop in the rope, then you take the end of the rope which is your 'rabbit' and pass it through the loop from the underside. Now you pass it *below* the rope above the loop and bring it back *over* the rope and into the loop again.

With a nylon rope you should always use a **bowline on the bight** (3). The technique is somewhat different here in that you double the rope on itself and, instead of returning the 'rabbit' to its hole, you loop it round the two free ends of the rope above the hole in the manner shown by the illustration.

I do not advise the reef knot for nylon ropes, although it is reasonably safe for use with a *kernmantel*. However, you can confidently put your trust in a **Prusik** knot (4) should you wish to attach a spliced loop of rope to your main line, and in the **Tarbuck** knot (5), which is a slightly more elaborate version of the bowline. Both these knots were developed by highly experienced climbers —the Austrian Dr Prusik and the British Ken Tarbuck—and have stood the test of time.

Finally, if you are faced with joining together two ropes of different sizes, you can use the **fisherman's knot** (6). It is very

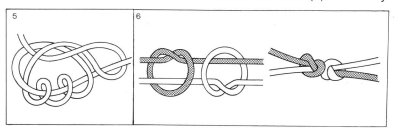

simple to tie but, with nylon, you would be well advised to take the
precaution of tying a **double fisherman**.

Krabs and pitons
Having acquired your rope, you should now begin to collect the
essential items of equipment that go with it. Firstly you will need
about half a dozen good **karabiners**, more commonly known as
'krabs'. There are several types of these on the market, fashioned
either in steel or in strong light alloy, but the krab I prefer most is
D-shaped. As you will see from the accompanying illustration,

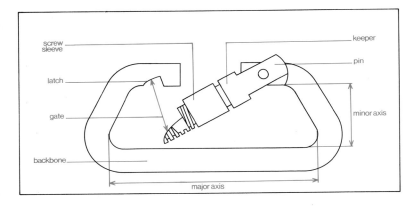

it is not unlike a padlock, having either a spring-loaded catch or
a screw sleeve on its curved part, which enables it to be opened
and then closed securely. On the straight part of the D there should
be stamped the breaking strain of the krab when the gate is
in the closed position. This should never be less than 4,500 lb,
but it is advisable to spend a little more money and buy krabs
with a minimum breaking strain of 7,500 lb (approximately
3,400 kg).

    As you will discover in due course, krabs have many uses. They
will enable you to secure a running rope or a loop either direct to
your waistline or to a loop attached to it. And, in like manner, they
may be used to secure ropes to *pitons* or belays. But this is only a
half of it. You will find that a krab will often get you out of difficulties
that could not be overcome otherwise. It is for this reason that
you should take great care of your krabs and inspect them regularly. Always make sure that the gates have not been weakened
and keep them well lubricated, applying a drop or two of thin
machine oil before and after each climb. In addition, examine the
metal for any signs of cracking. A krab that has been dropped
onto rock from some height may well be fractured.

Next you will require a set of **pitons**. These are basically large nails which may be driven into rock, ice or hard snow and which have holes at the blunt end for the attachment of ropes or krabs. *Pitons* are also used as artificial holds for the hands and feet.

There are, as you will gather from the illustration, many types of *piton* available, some of which have been designed for specific purposes. For use on most rocks, however, you need select only two types—the flat-bladed knife *piton* (**A**) and the channel *piton* (**B**) which has a U-shaped blade. Kit yourself out with a dozen of each variety, six of them having their rings in line with the shaft

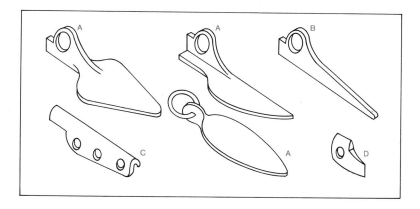

and six having rings at right angles to the shaft.

If you are proposing to climb with no more than half a dozen *pitons* it is best to thread them on a krab attached to your waistline. Larger numbers should be strung on a cord also attached to your waistline, but you must make certain they can be removed easily. I once had the misfortune to lose all my *pitons* off the loop whilst I was endeavouring to get one of them off—a not unusual experience for a beginner—and it taught me a salutary lesson. Thereafter I divided the loop into two sections by making a large knot in it (see illustration), so that if I ever lost the *pitons* in one section I should still have the remainder.

With your *pitons* you must, of course, have a *piton* hammer to drive them home. This should have a good, well-balanced head weighing not less than 8 oz and must be fastened to a loop of cord which you can sling either from your waistline or from your shoulder. This will prevent you from dropping the hammer, an accident that could land you in a pretty fix.

Never forget that your life and often those of others may depend upon how securely your *piton* is hammered home. Whenever possible try to plant it in a thin horizontal crack (avoid vertical cracks except as a last resort) and hammer it in until only the head and ring are visible. You can usually tell whether it is going to be secure or not by the sound it makes as you hammer. If it emits a clear, ringing note it is going to be all right, but if it sounds dull and flat it should not be trusted. In any case, you should always test your *piton* by attaching a krab to it, threading a piece of rope through and giving it as sharp a tug as you can manage (**1**).

Sometimes you may find it impossible to drive the *piton* right home. In such a case you must use a length of nylon tape, tying both ends round the head of the peg and then attaching your krab to the loop so formed. This substantially reduces the amount of leverage on the *piton* (**2**).

When driving *pitons* into the rock face try to do it at a downward angle (**3**), although an angle of 90 degrees to the rock face may suffice nearly as well. On no account drive the *piton* in at an upward angle (**4**) as it will almost certainly come adrift when subjected to a strain.

Pitons are removed by knocking them sideways backward and forward in much the same way as you would remove a large stubborn nail from a piece of timber. It is an unwritten law of climbing that they should be removed by the last man up, unless you intend to use the same *pitons* for your descent, in which case they are taken out by the last man down. However, you may come across certain rocks—usually those for training beginners—which have permanent *pitons* in place and these should always be left where they are. Likewise there are certain, comparatively easy climbs for which *pitons* are not permitted and, unless you want to make yourself thoroughly unpopular, you must abide by the rules.

Whoever does the removing must be sure to retain each *piton*. They are costly items these days—particularly if they are made from chrome alloy—and they can be used over and over again unless they become badly damaged. Quite apart from that, the wilful discarding of *pitons* will be heavily frowned upon by your fellow climbers. It is something that is just not done!

Many of today's more specialized *pitons* have been developed in the United States by climbers in the Yosemite. They are of a very high quality indeed—made of a strong, light alloy of chrome and molybdenum—and will certainly warrant your attention as soon as you graduate to more advanced climbing. For instance there is the **bong** (**C**) which derives its name from the deep, bell-like note it makes when struck. This is the heaviest of all *pitons* and has been designed for use in exceptionally wide cracks. By way of contrast there is the miniature 'realised ultimate reality *piton*' or **rurp** (**D**), to be employed in holes or shallow cracks which defy the penetration of knife and channel *pitons*.

There are, of course, other methods for securing a rope to the rock face. For instance, it is sometimes possible to wedge a krab securely in a crack and use this without the need for a *piton*. But

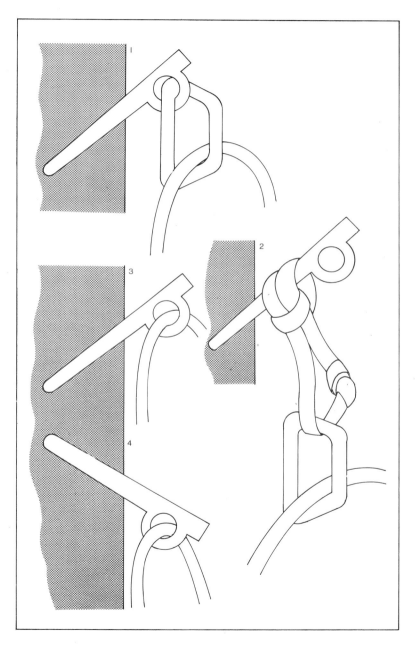

you should not indulge in this practice until you have gained
plenty of experience of the nature of rocks and the cracks that
form in them.

Other climbing aids

And then there is that useful gadget known as the artificial chockstone. Many years ago, climbers in Snowdonia discovered that
large nuts left behind by the builders of the Snowdon Railway
could also be wedged securely into cracks, after which a rope
could be passed through the centre hole once the thread had
been filed down to minimize abrasion. This led to the develop-
ment of the climber's **chock**. As you will observe, the hole is
now too narrow to permit that passage of a rope, but it will retain
a length of wire, which can be formed into a loop that in turn
supports the rope. Artificial chockstones, still referred to by
many climbers as nuts, are normally made of aluminium or brass
and take the form of short hexagonal bars in diameters up to
$1\frac{1}{4}$ inches or wedges.

The chockstone proper is a large rock or a boulder that has
become firmly wedged in a crack. It provides a ready and useful
means for a climber to anchor himself to the rock face by means
of what is known as a belay. You take a piece of rope as it comes
from your waistline, pass it around the chockstone and then bring
it back to your waistline and tie it securely. Conversely, if it is
possible to pass a loop over the chockstone, you use this in
conjunction with a krab. And now, providing you have selected
a good, firm chockstone, you will be in the position of anchor
man and thus able to help those behind you and hold them if
they should fall.

Belays may also be made with the help of rocky spikes, projections and solid, free-standing boulders. These are 'trapped' by
using a nylon sling attached to your climbing rope with a Prusik
knot and, when you become proficient, they may even be lassoed
from some distance. But you must always bear in mind that a rock,
unless it has been inspected closely or used to advantage by
previous climbers, may let you down by suddenly breaking away
or crumbling. For this reason it is always prudent to make two
belays whenever practicable. You can do this on your own or,
better still, you can ask the next man on the rope to make the
second belay.

In certain books on climbing I have seen trees recommended
as anchors for belays. I am loath to contradict the authors in
question, who are probably much better versed in techniques
than I am myself, but I could not disagree more with them on this
particular point and for very good reason. Trees that grow on
rocky ground, even though they may be large and appear sturdy,
nearly always have shallow roots. Indeed, their roots may often
spread across the surface of the rock in crablike manner and

never penetrate more than a few inches beneath it. In consequence these trees are liable to come away very suddenly under the strain of supporting several climbers on a rope. Some years back, whilst climbing in Bavaria, I witnessed a fatal accident from this cause and I have never put faith in a tree since.

Other techniques
One other technique you should practice and master before attempting more advanced rock climbing is that of the **abseil** or **rappel**. This is a method of making a quick descent by rope over rocks or ice and can save you a lot of time and effort on your way down.

You will need first to double your rope. You pass it through a *piton* or through the loop from a belay and, after making sure that the two ends are level, tie these together to prevent them from splaying outwards. You must also make sure that the doubled rope reaches right down to the place where you want to land. Now take a sling, which should be a spliced loop of No. 4 nylon rope about seven feet in circumference, twist it into a figure eight and slip your legs into the two smaller loops so formed (**1**). Clip a krab over the figure eight crossover and then draw the loops well up your thighs until they make a kind of chair(**2**). Pass the doubled rope through the krab and over your left shoulder, holding the rope in front of the krab with your left hand and the rope behind you with your right hand (**3**).

Now you must essay something which, believe me, will really test your nerve on the first two or three occasions. You walk backwards to the extreme edge of the cliff you propose to descend and then, braking the rope with your hands, continue walking backwards down the rock face (**4**). I can assure you it is not as terrifying as it sounds. Providing you don't grip the rope too tightly, thus burning your hands, you will find it quite a painless process. But I do advise you to practise abseiling of fairly short descents (10 to 15 feet) before tackling the big ones.

New methods of making abseils have been introduced in recent years, relying upon the use of a special device known as a **descendeur**, which is attached to the abseil loop's krab. One such *descendeur* is shaped like a trident and the abseil rope is wound round it three times between the prongs, thus producing a braking effect. The climber controls his descent by holding the rope in his right hand, at the same time grasping the *descendeur* in his left. This method does away with passing the abseil rope over the left shoulder and so avoids friction on the shoulder which, during long descents, can sometimes become painful. Another type of *descendeur*, known as the Fisher, is even better and easier to operate. As the illustration shows, it is not unlike a bottle opener in its appearance, consisting of a large loop or eye which is joined by a short shank to a smaller eye by which it is attached to the krab.

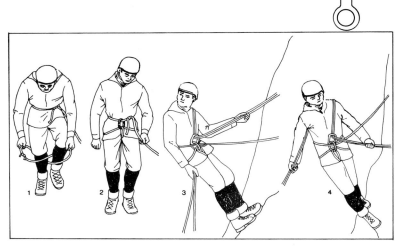

The rope is passed through the large eye and looped behind the shank in the manner shown. Both hands are then used to control the descent, one above and one below the *descendeur*.

The last piece of equipment with which you should become well acquainted is the **étrier**. This is simply a short portable ladder consisting of two short lengths of nylon rope spanned by two, three or four light alloy steps and joined to form a ring at the top end. On difficult climbs you should always carry two *étriers* with you and use them one after the other. First you hammer in a *piton* as high as possible and then clip the loop of the *étrier* onto it with a krab. Now you move up the rungs and hammer in another *piton* to which you attach the second *étrier*. You then retrieve *étrier* number one, fix it at a higher point and carry on with the same procedure until you reach a point where you can resume normal climbing. To assist you with this somewhat laborious method of

progress and to ensure that you do not drop an *étrier*, it is as well to carry a device known as a fifi hook, which is attached to the *étrier* and, by means of a thin cord, to your waistline.

Étriers have the disadvantage of being rather cumbersome, so climbers nowadays frequently dispense with them and use nylon webbing instead. This was employed by Commandos during the war and learning to climb on webbing formed a part of their training. It is extremely strong and very light, but care should be taken to see that it does not come in contact with a rubbing nylon rope as the resultant friction may induce melting.

The Prusik loop makes another good substitute for an *étrier* and, in addition, can be a godsend to any climber who finds himself in difficulties. It is a very simple device, consisting of a short length of No. 1 nylon rope joined with a Fisherman's knot, and it is attached to the main rope by means of a Prusik knot, which has the advantage that it can be slid along the rope when loose but will grip firmly as soon as any strain is placed on it. It is best to carry with you three or even four ready-made Prusik loops, ranging in circumference from four to seven feet.

Basic principles

Having discussed equipment at some length, let us now turn our attention to the basic principles of rock climbing. Though it is unlikely you will require a rope during the early stages, you should nevertheless carry one with you, even if your more experienced companions may be inclined to scoff, and you should also provide yourself with your waistline. This is effected by circling your waist with strong, thin cord six to ten times and tying it tight—but not too tight—with a reef knot. You could also attach two or three krabs to your waistline just to get the feel of them.

The rope is best slung around the shoulders in the manner of a bandolier. Take a 100-foot length of No. 4 and coil it twenty times, each coil having the same diameter, then fasten the two ends with a slip knot. Should you require to use the rope, be sure to unwind it one coil at a time, thus avoiding any risk of tangling.

The simplest form of rock to climb is known technically as a **glacis** and seldom has a gradient of more than 30 degrees. In most cases you will be able to walk up it normally, though you may have to resort to using your hands on occasions, but do not despise it because of this, as it will teach you a few elementary lessons on how to keep both your head and your balance.

From *glacis* you can now proceed to **slab**, which varies from 30 to 75 degrees, choosing a gritstone rock if you can find one. This is where you will need an experienced companion to help you and it may be advisable to rope yourself to him, in which case you should allow for a good length between the two of you, certainly not less than 30 feet. When you come to more difficult climbing it is usual to allow for as much as 100 feet.

Inspect the rock face for possible holds, then reach for one at about eye level, draw yourself up a foot or two and place the toes of both feet into another, lower hold. Remove your hands, make sure you are balanced perfectly on your feet, then repeat the process. Never remain stationary for any length of time when using a toe hold or you will be almost certain to develop a leg-shake, which is quite an unnerving experience. If you want to take a brief rest, do so at a place where you can put your heels down. You will find that perfect stationary balance can be maintained just by pressing the palms of your hands against the rock.

As you progress with your slab climbing you are almost bound to come across one of those awkward spots where you will find a ledge at waist level and will have to lift both feet onto it. You will now have to resort to a tedious procedure known as a mantel-shelf move. Placing the palms of both hands firmly on the ledge, press down hard until you can raise one foot to where you hands are. Slowly raise yourself on this foot, at the same time straightening up, and you will then be able to step on the ledge with your other foot. There is nothing particularly dangerous about mantel-shelving, but you will find it exasperating and sometimes almost impossible if your abdominal muscles are inclined to be flabby. I therefore suggest that you practise it at home, using the top of a heavy table or a work bench as your 'shelf', or in a gymnasium on a vaulting horse. I used to do this several times each day at the start of my climbing career and I got my muscles in trim after a very short space of time.

Jamming
We have so far dealt with simple holds, which are virtually no more than shallow natural steps on the rock face. Now you should have a go at crack holds, where you use deep vertical fissures in the rock to aid your progress. Since these afford no horizontal support for the feet or hands, you must resort to a method known as jamming. Hand jamming may be effected in various ways, as the accompanying illustrations demonstrate. The basic jam merely consists of placing your hand sideways into the fissure and expanding it either by drawing the fingers up or by forcing your thumb across your palm. It is possible to jam without any holds in the crack whatsoever. A more elaborate hold is the hand and elbow jam, which results in a stronger grip. Both hands may be used, either inside the crack or pulling outward on the edges, and occasions when the crack narrows above and below forming a sort of hole you will find a fist jam useful.

Foot or foot jamming is a little bit more complicated and can sometimes be painful, as indeed are some hand jams. The basic method is shown in the illustration, whilst the layback move, in which you use the friction of your feet against the rock face, may also be seen. Whatever you do, you must take the utmost care

Jamming

1 Basic Foot
2 Layback using foot and hand jamming
3 Backing using knee jamming
4 Basic Hand
5 Hand and Elbow
6 Double Hand Jam
7 Fist Jam
8 Backing up
9 Bridging

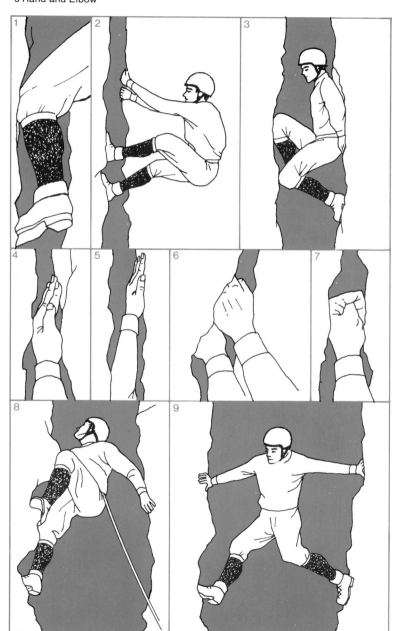

not to get a hand or a foot firmly wedged. If this should ever happen, don't struggle, as this may result in an injury. Stay where you are and get another climber to help you.

Body jamming is nearly always imperative when tackling wide fissures in the rock, known as chimneys. If there is sufficient width they are best climbed by what is known as the backing up method when you use not only your hands and feet but also a large portion of your back. Otherwise you will have to resort to whatever technique appears to be the most suitable, such as the use of back and knees or the bridging method, which entails spread-eagling yourself across the gap.

Chimneys
Chimneys can be absolute hell at times and I have known them reduce some hardy climbers almost to the point of tears! Sometimes an occasion will arise when, having progressed quite comfortably up a chimney for some distance, you will find yourself thwarted by a complete lack of holds for the next few feet. In this case you will have to resort to a combined effort with the companion immediately behind you. Once you have anchored yourself firmly you get him to scramble up your back and perch himself on your shoulders, when he will then probably be able to find a secure hold and pull you up. When climbing in the Dolomites some years ago, I was forced to use this method in triplicate, with

a third companion standing on the shoulders of the second. It was a successful move but not one that I would care to repeat.

Until you are really professional you should not attempt overhangs. Most of them can be avoided by discontinuing your present direction of climb and moving horizontally across the rock face to a spot where your ascent will not be obstructed. This technique is known as traversing and is simple enough to accomplish where you have horizontal cracks stretching for some distance, as is so often the case with gritstone. You should make sure that there are cracks for your feet as well as your hands and you can then proceed sideways along the face of the rock. Traversing with hand holds only is hazardous as well as tiring and should not be attempted except as a last resort.

Before concluding this chapter on rock climbing, let me again stress the value of practising all complicated moves in places where you are not so likely to come unstuck and injure yourself. You should not experience much difficulty in locating outcrops of rock where you will find chimneys starting at ground level and there will doubtless be a few overhangs from which you could take a tumble without doing yourself much harm. Most of the rock climbing schools can provide such training grounds and you will find it well worth your while to spend a little money and make use of them. In no other sport does the old maxim of 'practice makes perfect' apply so aptly as in climbing.

5 ON TOP OF THE WORLD

Rock climbing may be enjoyed in nearly every country in the world and there are few people who do not live within fairly easy reach of a suitable cliff or outcrop on which to learn and practice. But with the high peaks it is different. Mountains there are in plenty, of course; you have only to look at a relief map of any continent to realize that. The only trouble is that most of them are virtually inaccessible to ninety-five per cent of the world's population except by taking a long and expensive journey.

It is for this reason that the European Alps, and particularly those of Switzerland, have remained the most popular mountaineering centres for well over a century. Even in the days when there was only surface travel they could be reached from most of the capitals of Europe in less than twenty-four hours and now, in this era of jet aircraft, you can leave New York at eight in the evening and be in Switzerland in time for breakfast the following day. Though you may live much closer to the Yukon, the Yosemite or the Andes, it would be preferable for you to start your mountaineering in the Alps for a number of very good reasons.

In the first place, the Alps have now become highly organized. Recognized routes to the summits of most peaks have been carefully planned and described in numerous readily available guidebooks published by the Swiss Alpine Club and others. Secondly, there is seldom any need to bivouac in the mountains—unless you are attempting a monumental climb or a high-level tour of the peaks—since there are several hundred alpine huts and refuges where you may spend the night or shelter in bad weather. Thirdly, the climbing centres in Switzerland, Italy and France can always supply you with a qualified guide who will not only lead you safely wherever you want to go but will also instruct you in the art of mountaineering. And lastly, most important of all, the mountain rescue services in the Alps are some of the finest in the world.

All mountaineers must acquire certain special skills but, before describing these in detail, let me reiterate what I have said earlier, that climbing at high altitudes imposes physical strains that you will not have encountered when fell walking or scrambling on the rocks. The higher you go the more rarefied the atmosphere becomes, so that you will find it increasingly difficult to breathe and your heart begins to beat more quickly. It will thus be necessary to slacken speed and to take more frequent rests.

I have found that one way of overcoming this drawback to a certain extent is to select as your headquarters a village that itself lies at a pretty high altitude, say at 6,000 feet or more. By the time you have remained here for two or three days, in the meantime taking fairly strenuous walks in the vicinity, you will have largely acclimatized yourself to the atmospheric conditions and be better equipped physically for the climbs ahead.

Another hazard that you do not find described in most textbooks is mountain sickness. This terrifying malady, which can afflict even the strongest and fittest of individuals, strikes suddenly and has been the cause of many accidents. Doctors have been unable to explain it satisfactorily, but it is generally believed to be caused by changes in the blood occasioned by lack of oxygen at high altitudes. The victim grows pale and cold, frequently vomits and is assailed by fears which may eventually drive him berserk. Luckily mountain sickness is not a common complaint, but you should be on your guard in case you are one of the unfortunates. Should you begin to show signs of any of the earlier symptoms, inform your guide or your companions at once and make arrangements for quitting the party immediately. The others won't consider you 'chicken' but will appreciate your concern for their own safety.

What makes a mountaineer?

In order to be a proficient mountaineer, you must satisfy yourself that you possess the following qualities:

1 Sound health, physical fitness and a capacity for endurance despite weather conditions and sudden changes of temperature.
2 Perfect acquaintance with all types of climbing equipment.
3 A good knowledge of how mountains are constructed and the types of weather that you may encounter at high altitudes.
4 Map-reading ability and a knack for spotting the most likely routes across rock, snow and ice.
5 Skill in rope management on rock, snow and ice and in difficult conditions and emergencies.
6 A capacity for moving safely and as quickly as possible over hazardous or difficult ground.
7 A knowledge of crevasse rescue procedure.
8 An ability to get on well with your climbing companions and to safeguard them as a party.
9 Thorough experience of abseiling.
10 A knowledge of the conditions that favour avalanches and of how to foresee possible avalanches and take evasive action.

Taking for granted that you can comply with the first qualification on this list, let us now turn to item 2. You will have acquired most of the basic equipment you will need in the course of fell walking and rock climbing, though you must now be sure that you possess a set of crampons, for these are essential in the high Alps. However, you will need a few important additions for mountaineering.

Snow goggles are of vital importance, otherwise the glare from snow and glaciers can very easily produce a very painful and often dangerous condition known as snow blindness. Buy a good lightweight pair—don't be tempted into getting cheap ones—and make sure the lenses are made of tinted, reinforced glass and never of plastic. If you normally have to wear spectacles, ask your oculist to supply the correct lenses.

You will also need a special anti-sun oil or cream (those used

Alpine clothing. Note helmet and goggles, leather mitts, long cagoule, breeches and zipped gaiters, alpine boots and large unframed rucksack with crampons

by sunbathers are not effective enough) and this should be applied thoroughly to every part of the body exposed, taking particular care not to forget the nostrils, the underchin, the backs of the ears and the inside of the arms. Lip salve is equally important and should be used frequently whilst climbing in the sun.

Alpinism causes intense sweating with consequent dehydration so you will need plenty to drink. Take with you a large plastic water bottle of about one-litre capacity and add a glass of wine to the water, which will give it wonderful thirst-quenching properties. I am not in favour of drinking mountain spring water (for reasons previously stated) or melted snow, but these should not affect your stomach if you allow them to warm up in your flask first.

Some mountaineers invariably carry a small aneroid barometer with them and you will find this valuable for predicting approaching changes in the weather and for giving you a fairly accurate reading of your altitude.

Finally, don't forget your headgear, because sunstroke is very prevalent in the Alps. A light felt or straw hat with a sensibly wide brim may be worn during the earlier part of your climb, with the addition of a neckerchief if the sun is very strong, but you should

Walking across a glacier. Depending on
the weather conditions, make sure you
wear crampons on your climbing boots

carry your helmet with you (strapped to the top of your rucksack)
and exchange this for your hat when you reach precipitous ground.

For most climbs it will not be necessary to take along camping
equipment, though I strongly advise you to add a short sleeping
bag to the contents of your rucksack just in case you are benighted
or hampered by a storm. The type known in French as a *duvet
court* is the best. It weighs only a few ounces and, when worn,
comes up to chest level, being secured over your shoulders by
tapes.

Glaciers
Let us now turn to item 3 on the preceding list. A thorough knowledge of mountains and accompanying weather phenomena can
only be acquired by long experience, but it would be advisable to
read a few good books on the subject nevertheless. However, you
should acquaint yourself as soon as possible with the structure
and behaviour of glaciers, since these exhibit unique features
you will not have encountered before.

A glacier is in fact a river of ice, which flows slowly down the
side of a mountain at a speed of from 5 to 20 feet a year towards

a spot where the temperature is sufficiently high and constant to
melt it, thus forming countless rivulets which merge into streams
that in turn become rivers.

Unlike most orthodox rivers, glaciers do not originate from
springs. Their source is the snow which falls on high mountains
and which, as it is dragged downwards by its own weight and the
force of gravity, compacts itself into ice which may be several
hundred feet in depth. This snow is known in French as *névé* and
in German as *firn*.

Under the weight of the ice, the rocky ground on which it lies quite often breaks away or shifts its position. This sets up stresses in the ice and produces cracks, varying in width from a few inches to a considerable number of feet, which are called *crevasses*. Since these nearly always extend from top to bottom of the glacier, they present a constant danger to persons climbing on the ice and have been the cause of many fatalities and serious injuries. They are particularly dangerous in the colder months of the year and after heavy snowfalls when they are covered and obscured by snow bridges. These, providing they have frozen solidly, can be helpful by providing a means of crossing the *crevasse*, but they are always likely to give way without warning. Treat them with the respect they deserve and always heed the advice of a local guide if you are in any doubt.

In any case, I strongly advise the use of a rope for all parties attempting to traverse a glacier that is known to be dangerous. I am fully aware that many climbers will deride such a precaution, but I prefer to abide by the advice given time and time again by the Alpine guides who, after all, are professionals. Roping up, when climbing over snow and ice, is quite different from that used in rock climbing. The distance between each member of the party on ascent should never exceed 40 feet and, when descending, it should be reduced to between 5 and 10 feet.

Another, more fearsome kind of *crevasse* is known as a *berg-schrund* and is usually found on the side of a glacier, the river bank as it were. Here one lip of the crack may be a considerable number of feet above the other and it is impossible to span the gap by taking a simple stride. You can, of course, get across if there happens to be a reliable snow bridge, but you will still be faced with a wall of ice that you must scale. My advice is to avoid the *bergschrund* whenever you can and, if you must cross it, do so at its narrowest point. In any event, you should *never* attempt such a crossing alone.

Glaciers are described as being 'dry' when they are free from snow—usually in the summer months—and 'wet' when they are covered with snow, which may even persist throughout the summer on the upper reaches. In very hot weather the surface of the ice will melt towards midday and the resultant slush begins to freeze in the late afternoon making the surface very slippery and treacherous. It is therefore advizable to effect your crossing well before noon in such circumstances.

On simple glaciers, which have shallow gradients and present few hazards, you will be able to move quite comfortably with ordinary climbing boots. Otherwise you must resort to crampons and you should make sure that these fit securely and are neither too large nor too small for your boots. You will find that they cause little or no discomfort, since the plate of the crampon is hinged at the instep and thus permits flexibility of the foot. If there is a fair amount of snow about, it may become wedged between the spikes

of the crampons, producing a dangerous condition known as 'balling up', which prevents the spikes making a grip. So be sure to check for this at regular intervals and to clean away any snow that may have become impacted.

The bottom end of a glacier is termed the snout and immediately below it is the *moraine*, a veritable sea of boulders and fragments of rock which the moving glacier has brought down with it through the ages. Occasionally you will come across a glacier that is bifurcated and has two snouts. This will probably have a projection where the split occurs, known as a spur, and a secondary *moraine* or medial *moraine*. Other features of glaciers include *seracs*, which are detached pinnacles of ice (sometimes rising

to a height of 100 feet or more) and which, since they tend to collapse suddenly, should be kept at a safe distance; and icefalls, where the glacier is a mass of cracks and *crevasses* piled with the crumbled remains of *seracs*. Sometimes these are useful for learning ice-climbing techniques but, generally speaking, these should also be avoided.

Though a single rope is quite adequate for glacier work, there is something to be said for having two for additional protection, in which case the second rope should be of a different colour from the other. However, whether you adopt this method or not, you should see to it that each number of your party carries a coil of some 40 or 50 feet of No. 4 nylon as a spare. Incidentally, I regard

Previous pages: North face of the Cima
di Rosso in Switzerland showing a
typical *bergschrund*

nylon rope as a 'must' for ice and snow climbing, since it is unaffected by wet weather.

Some climbers make a loop in the rope at arm's length in front of them, which is useful if they should happen to fall in a *crevasse*, but it is a much better idea to take along two ready-made Prusik loops with you, already attached to the rope. These can be tucked into your waistline to prevent them from tripping you up.

When moving across the ice, make sure that the rope is neither too slack or too tight, otherwise a sharp tug may result in a nasty accident. Let it dip to some extent but keep it well off the surface. You will find this difficult to maintain until you have mastered the art of simultaneous movement, which is one of the fundamentals of all alpinism. It is absolutely essential that you and your companions move as a team, all stepping forward at the same time and pace. This technique needs a lot of practice and you and your fellow-climbers will find it really worthwhile to acquire the rhythm, first on grassy slopes and then over easy stretches of snow, before setting off together on your climb.

On dangerous glacier crossings the orthodox waistline may slip off if you ever have the misfortune to topple into a *crevasse* upside down, particularly if you have narrow hips or have begun to develop 'middle-age spread'. You should therefore take the additional precaution of attaching the rope with krabs to a thigh loop and a chest loop. As an alternative, many climbers now favour a *klettergürtel*, or climbing harness. This replaces both the waistline and the loops and also minimizes the risk of injury to the chest or internal organs in the event of a severe fall.

In a party of three or four, the most experienced climber must always lead, with the next most experienced one going last, just in case you have to go in reverse. When descending, however, it is imperative that the most experienced man is last, since he may have to act as an anchor if those in front of him slip.

It is in circumstances like this that the ice-axe really comes into its own. Glaciers offer no firm protuberances or projections around which a rope may be belayed, so the axe must be employed in lieu. If the surface of the glacier is covered in soft snow, the axe should be driven shaft downwards for at least half its length and the rope belayed beneath its head. Otherwise you must drive the pick into the ice as far as it will go and make sure that the rope is belayed around the head and on the pick side of it. You should always carry your ice-axe at the ready so that you can drive it in immediately any emergency arises or when you are called upon to act as an anchor. To prevent the shaft slipping through your grip, you should use a leather wrist loop.

Crevasses

When you come to a *crevasse*, stop at once and make a careful survey of it. If it extends for only a short distance, it is always best to make a detour to avoid it. Failing that, try to find a point where it is narrow enough for you to be able to cross in a single stride. When you are unable to do this, you may find it possible to jump the distance. In such a case, warn the other members of the party so that they can anchor themselves firmly and make sure that the foothold is firm at both your landing and your take-off point. Then take in a few coils of slack rope and release them when you are in mid-air. Pitch yourself forward and roll over, away from the *crevasse*, as you land. You will in all probability be wearing crampons, so be certain to land on both feet simultaneously, otherwise you will find the shock painful.

If you are forced to cross a snow bridge there is one golden rule you and your party must remember and that is never to venture on it more than one man at a time. But before attempting any crossing, you must examine the bridge thoroughly, probing it with an ice-axe and even hitting it if necessary in order to determine its consistency. The leader should then be the first over, whilst the others act as anchors and keep the rope taut. If the leader is at all doubtful, he must crawl across on his hands and

knees, thus distributing his weight over a greater area, gripping his ice-axe firmly and keeping it at right angles to the line of the *crevasse*. Once across he must belay the rope with the axe and not let the others cross until this is done to his satisfaction. This is because snow bridges still have an awkward habit of collapsing even after they have withstood the strain of one or two people crossing.

You will find that climbing in the high mountains will be largely a matter of rock-climbing, especially at lower altitudes, but as soon as you are faced with snow and ice you will have to adopt new techniques. Generally speaking, snow does not present too many problems, although you must always be on the alert for patches that have become encrusted with a layer of ice and you should avoid anything that looks like a deep drift. Snow ridges make comparatively easy going, unless they are raked by strong winds. If this is the case you should shorten the length of rope between each climber to no more than four or five feet, keeping close together and moving slowly and with caution.

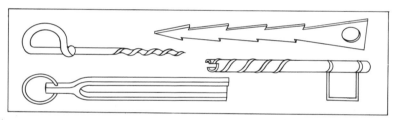

Ice, on the other hand, is quite different. An ice wall should be treated with even greater respect than a difficult rock face and the great secret is to use your brain, tackling the ascent at a slow pace and never losing your patience. You will need special ice *pitons* (see above) where the wall is sheer and you will find nylon webbing very handy.

Step-cutting
Never tackle a climb on ice or hard snow until you have learnt how to make steps with your ice-axe. This is not such a difficult procedure as you might think but, like every other specialized mountaineering technique, it needs a lot of practice. The most important thing about step-cutting is being able to keep a perfect balance, for you will need to wield your axe from an erect position. In most cases it is necessary to chip away only enough snow or ice as will suffice to make a hold large enough for the toe part of your boot to be inserted but, on a long and tedious climb, it is advisable to make a few larger holes at intervals, in order to form a platform on which both feet may be rested, thus providing you with a breather. Whenever possible I try to avoid cutting steps one

Three methods of cutting steps in ice.
Note the need for a firm anchorage
when in a dangerous position

above the other, since this makes climbing much too strenuous.
It is infinitely better to arrange them in a zig-zag pattern which,
whilst taking longer, provides you with an infinitely easier climb.

When the ice wall above you begins to look too formidable or
resolves itself into an overhang, you will have to make steps
horizontally to traverse right or left to a more likely spot. However,
providing you have surveyed the wall thoroughly before attempting to tackle it, traversing should not be necessary. You should
avoid this move whenever possible, since cutting steps simply for
traversing purposes uses up a lot of valuable energy.

Crossing deep snow that has been
exposed to strong sunlight can be
hazardous

And that brings me to an important point. Though step-cutting
may appear to be easy, it can be extremely tiring if carried out
for any length of time, particularly in high altitude conditions. This
tiredness is an extremely bad thing, since it can result in the step-
cutter not only losing his confidence but also becoming careless
and endangering others besides himself. It is better for climbers
to abandon a climb rather than to allow themselves to get in this
condition. No matter where you are on a mountain, the moment
you begin to feel signs of exhaustion have the sense—and courage
—to call it a day.

Weather hazards and avalanches
Weather conditions in the Alps can sometimes present more
problems than any of the rock faces and ice cliffs you are likely
to encounter. I have discussed in an earlier chapter how to fore-
cast approaching changes in the weather from cloud formations
and this system still holds good in areas where there are high
mountains, though you should remember that the changes usually
occur much more rapidly than they do in hilly regions. You should
never set out on a long climb if there is much *Stratus* about, nor if
you observe dark thunderclouds congregating over the summits.
Wind direction is also significant in the Alps. If the wind is from
the north or north-east it portends fine, clear weather, but winds
from the west and south-west are usually indicative of rain and a
blow coming straight from the south will almost certainly cause
the snow to melt and thus put you in danger of avalanches.

It takes a lot of experience to be able to predict avalanches with
any degree of accuracy; indeed, the art is like a sixth sense with
many seasoned mountaineers. I used to go climbing with a
wonderful old guide from Zermatt who assured me that he could
'smell' avalanches hours before they actually occurred and,
although I had the temerity to disbelieve him at first, it was not
long before he afforded me proof of his 'supernatural' power.

Unfortunately the average mountaineer is not so gifted and the
best advice I can offer here is to be distrustful always of sudden
spells of unusually warm weather coming hard on the heels of
cold periods and to take particular care when climbing after heavy
rainfalls, which are the major cause of stone and rock avalanches.
Listen keenly for the distinctive sound of avalanches in the
vicinity and keep a good lookout for the tracks of previous avalanches. Above all, take heed of any warnings from the local
population. These people know far more about their prevailing
weather conditions than you do.

Climbers themselves have frequently been the cause of serious
avalanches in the past, usually inadvertently but on some occasions as the result of crass stupidity, so it is as well to take the
following precautions. Never on any account walk on snow that
is close to the edge of a path or overhangs the lip of a precipice.

If you are forced to cross deep snow that has been exposed to strong sunlight or a recent rainstorm, tread very carefully and try to avoid sliding. Do not run or jump on snow unless it is absolutely necessary and refrain from dislodging boulders or large stones. In tricky places it is even advisable not to shout loudly and, above all, don't indulge in any schoolboy pranks such as snowballing. Two friends of mine were badly injured and nearly lost their lives in an avalanche started off by the throwing of a snowball no more than eight ounces in weight. Finally, if you should feel the snow or ground beginning to give way under your feet get off it as quickly as you can.

Fortunately avalanches of any size are fairly rare and are seldom responsible for more than five per cent of the accidents that occur in the Alps each year. Even so, the accident rate continues to remain high (with over 300 climbers being killed or injured annually) and it is regrettable that a high proportion of them are due to lack of experience or to plain foolishness. At the same time, prompt rescue operations have kept the toll much lower than it might have been and I should like to end this chapter with some advice on what to do in case of emergency. I shall deal only with simple rescue techniques, since it is best to leave full-scale operations in the hands of those who have been specially trained to cope with them.

Rescue techniques

Falls are, of course, the most frequent mishaps, though a climber held securely on his rope doesn't often suffer much more than a winding and a few bruises. It is nevertheless vital to bring him back to level ground as quickly as possible or to lower him to safety, whichever is more practicable. In either case he must be hauled up or dropped down in a vertical position, otherwise he stands the chance of collecting further injuries, and this is where his Prusik loop can prove of utmost value. If he can manage to get his feet into these they will hold him securely and he need use his hands only for steadying himself. Should the fallen climber be prone on a ledge or hanging horizontally, a krab will have to be lowered to him on a separate rope. He should then pass this rope under his armpits and make a loop with the krab, when hauling on the second rope will then bring him into position from

A

B

which he will be able to grasp the main rope (**A**).

This rescue technique will be found comparatively simple where the victim is conscious and able to assist himself. But if he becomes jammed—which often happens with falls into *crevasses*—it will be necessary for another member of the party to come and aid him (**B**). Here again the Prusik loops can be used to great advantage, although *étriers*, if carried, will do equally as well.

If you haven't any of this equipment with you, a rescuer may be lowered by means of the pulley system. An axe is driven firmly into the snow or ice and the end of a rope tied to the shaft just below the head. The rope is then slipped through a krab attached to the climber's waistline or thigh loop and gradually paid out by an anchored member of the party as the climber slowly descends, gripping the wall with his crampons. Then, providing he has no serious back injuries, a triple bowline may be tied round the fallen man and attached to the hauling rope, but in certain cases some kind of improvised stretcher may be needed. This may take the form of a *tragsitz* or carrier seat, which is the only type of rescue equipment that can be carried in a rucksack without increasing the weight unduly.

When a climber's injuries are serious enough to demand the assistance of a mountain rescue team, help should be summoned as quickly as possible. Provided you have made your intentions clear at the point of your departure, the local guides will no doubt have been observing your progress through fieldglasses and will be quick to notice any distress signals. If not, it is up to one or two members of your party to go in search of assistance but, unless circumstance prohibit it, one climber should always remain with the injured man. If this can't be done, he should be taken to a place of shelter, made as comfortable as possible and covered with as many items of clothing as the others can spare. Provided he isn't suffering from internal injuries, a water bottle should be left within his reach. And if you can manage to light a fire nearby—but not too near—it will serve the double purpose of keeping the victim warm (if only psychologically) and of identifying his location after nightfall.

Maybe you will think I am ending this short work on climbing with a note of depression. But I must stress once again the importance of taking the sport seriously and of knowing what to do in case of accident. Every climber worth his salt should know how to set about his task safely, how to keep his head in an emergency and how to give first aid. He must learn that all climbs are to be respected with reverence and that they, having been accorded this courtesy, will respect their climbers in turn.

Stick to the rules, be prudent enough not to attempt anything that you feel might be beyond you and you will still be climbing at a ripe old age.

GLOSSARY

Abseil A means of making a quick, steep descent with a double rope

A cheval Progressing by straddling a ridge

Acorns Types of artificial chockstones

Aiguille A sharp-pointed, needle-like rock

Aneroid A type of barometer, also used for altitude reading

Anorak A hooded garment, resistant to wind and rain

Avalanche A sudden fall of rock, stones, snow or ice

Balling up Hard snow wedged on crampons; a dangerous condition

Belay An anchor point when climbing

Bergschrund A gap or crevasse between two different levels

Bivouac A temporary camp

Bong A *piton* for inserting in large cracks, so-called because of the noise it makes when struck

Buttress An isolated rocky mass

Cagoule An anorak that reaches below the knees

Cairn A pile of stones indicating a summit or marking a route

Chest-tie A loop around the chest used instead of a waist-loop

Chimney A wide vertical fissure in rock or ice

Chockstone A large stone or boulder jammed in a crack or chimney that can be used as a belay point

Clinkers Edge nails on a climbing boot, usually made of soft iron

Col A mountain pass

Couloir A steep, deep and often narrow gulley

Crampon Metal spikes on a frame that can be attached to a climbing boot

Crevasse A vertical fissure in a glacier

Dagger A *piton* that provides a hand-hold or a foothold

Descendeur A metal ring used in abseiling

Diédre An 'open book' formation made by two angled rock faces

Dôme A rounded summit, usually snow-covered

Duvet A down-filled overgarment or sleeping-bag

Espadrilles Rope-soled lightweight boots

Ètrier A short ladder with rope sides and alloy rungs

Fell A hill or moor

Fifi-hook A means of attaching an étrier to a karabiner

Friction Adhering to rock by the pressure of hands and feet

Funnel An ice-wall in a gulley, not to be used for glissading

Glacier A slow-moving river of ice

Glissade A means of sliding down an ice slope

Guide When used of a person, a professional climber

Holds Natural cracks or projections on the rock face for supporting hands and feet

Ice axe An axe for cutting steps in ice or hand snow, for anchoring, for maintaining balance and for controlling speed on a glissade

Icefall A large area of a glacier that has broken away

Jamming Thrusting hands and feet into large cracks to aid ascent

Jug-handle A large incut hold in rock that will take a climber's full weight

Karabiner A metal snap-close ring with a hinged spring-loaded gate. (Usually known as a 'krab')

Kernmantel A rope with an inner core protected by an outer sheath

Kletterschuhen Lightweight climbing boots with soft soles

Leeper A type of *piton* of American design

Live hand A belayed climber's hand that is closest to the following moving climber

Mantelshelf A horizontal ledge on a rock face

Moraine Debris brought down by a glacier to its foot

Névé Snow on the head of a glacier that is turning into ice

Nuts Small metal artificial chockstones

Overhang Rock jutting out over a vertical face

PA's Lightweight climbing boots

Pendule A horizontal *abseil* effected by a sideways swing

Piton A metal peg that is hammered into rock or ice and will then support a rope, an étrier or a hold

Rake A diagonal ledge on a rock face

Rappel Another word for an *abseil*

Ridge A narrow rock spine on which it is possible to walk or straddle

Roof The underside of an overhang

Rurp The smallest type of *piton* to be used in emergency in shallow cracks

Saddle A depression on a ridge

Scree A mass of broken stones or slate

Sérac A pinnacle of ice usually on a glacier

Snout The lowest end of a glacier

Snowbridge A bridge of snow over a crevasse

Straddling Standing athwart in a chimney or proceeding *à cheval* along a ridge

Swaging Joining two wire ropes together by squeezing a metal sheath over the ends

Tarbuck A knot devised by Kenneth Tarbuck that will absorb energy during a fall

Thread belay A natural hole in a rock through which a tape or rope may be threaded

Top rope An extra rope lowered down to assist a climber in an emergency

Traverse Moving horizontally across a face or slope

Tricounis Sharp climbing nails mounted on a metal plate

V-chimney An open chimney not more than five feet wide and narrowing at the bottom

Verglas A layer of ice caused by freezing mist or rain, sometimes called 'black ice' and very perilous

Vibrams Boot soles made from moulded rubber or hard plastic

Waist-loop A length of rope wound round the waist to which is attached the climbing rope and a belay

Windslab A hard crust of snow blown by the wind on top of old snow

Further reading list

Banks, M.
Commando Climber, London 1955

Blackshaw, A.
Mountaineering, New York 1968, London 1970

Bonington, C.
I Chose to Climb, London 1966, New York 1966

Engel, C. A.
A History of Mountaineering in the Alps, London 1950

Ingram, J. A.
Fellcraft, London 1965, New York 1965

Lovelock, J.
Climbing, London 1971

Lunn, Sir A.
A Century of Mountaineering, London 1957, New York 1958

Milne, M. (ed.)
The Book of Modern Mountaineering, London 1968, New York 1968

Milner, D.
Rock for Climbing, London 1950

Peacock, T. A. H.
Mountaineering, London 1941, New York 1941

Pyatt, E. C. & Noyce, W.
British Crags and Climbers, London 1952

Styles, S.
Rock and Rope, London 1967

Unsworth, W.
Because It Is There, London 1968

The Book of Rock Climbing, London 1968

Wright, J. E. B.
The Technique of Mountaineering, London 1965, New York 1965

Young, G. W.
Mountain Craft, London 1945

INDEX